T0266987

Screen-Free Family Activities

Things to Do Together at Home, around Town, and in Nature

ZAZU NAVARRO

Illustrations by **Teresa Cebrián**

Translated by Allie Hauptman

Skyhorse Publishing

Library of Congress Cataloging-in-Publication Data is available on file.

Cover design by Teresa Cebrián & David Ter-Avanesyan
Cover illustrations by Teresa Cebrián
Interior design by Teresa Cebrián
English edition editor: Nicole Frail

Print ISBN: 978-1-5107-6715-7

Printed in China

To all the families helping love grow with time, patience, and dedication.

Visit the author's website for the downloadable content referenced throughout the book.

www.aprendiendoconmontessori.com

IN OUR FAMILY

 WE LOVE people
more than any <u>screen</u>.

We believe in the POWER
of a real live smile.

 We are guided by WHERE WE PUT
OUR FEET and not where we put
our phone.

 When we have to WAIT, we draw
on placemats, and clap and chat.

If we are thinking of someone, we do not
hesitate to go KNOCK ON THEIR DOOR.

HA HA
HA HA
We share JOKES that make our
hearts buzz and not our phones.

WE SMILE, we surprise each other
with silly faces.

And above all,

 WE SPEND TIME TOGETHER.

How to read this book

Interesting note about the activity. Something that surprised us.

Number to help find activities easily

Minimum age for each activity

Recommended season

❄ Winter

✿ Spring

☀ Summer

🍁 Autumn

Approximate time it will take to complete the activity

Description of the activity

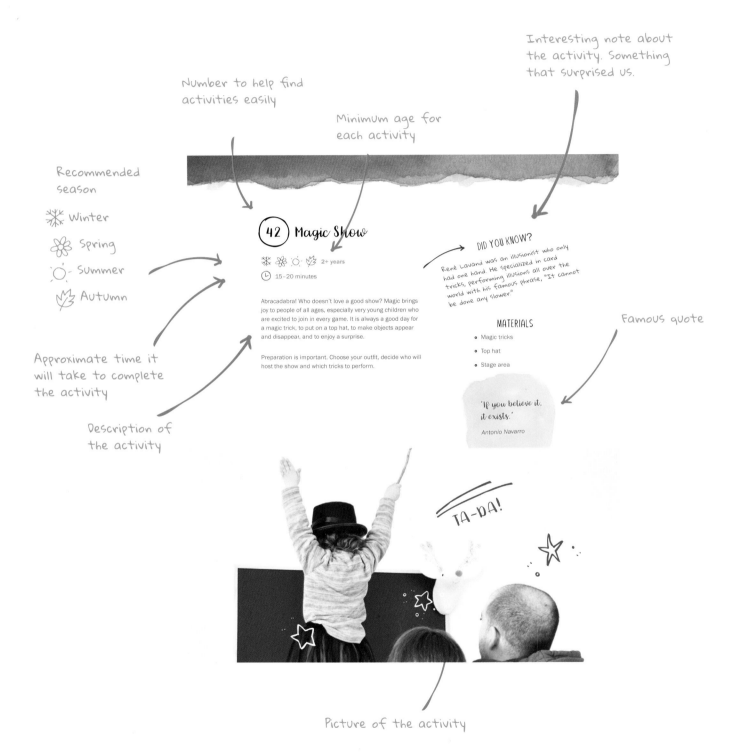

(42) Magic Show

❄ ✿ ☀ 🍁 2+ years

🕐 15–20 minutes

Abracadabra! Who doesn't love a good show? Magic brings joy to people of all ages, especially very young children who are excited to join in every game. It is always a good day for a magic trick, to put on a top hat, to make objects appear and disappear, and to enjoy a surprise.

Preparation is important. Choose your outfit, decide who will host the show and which tricks to perform.

DID YOU KNOW?

René Lavand was an illusionist who only had one hand. He specialized in card tricks, performing illusions all over the world with his famous phrase, "It cannot be done any slower."

MATERIALS

- Magic tricks
- Top hat
- Stage area

Famous quote

'If you believe it, it exists.'

Antonio Navarro

TA-DA!

Picture of the activity

6

Using **inclusive language** is very important when expressing ourselves.

Screen-Free Family Activities is designed for all families, no two of which are the same. There are tons of activities in this book, and you don't have to do them in order: this is a guide, a great resource to help step away from screens.

The activities are divided into **three different environments**: at home, around town, and in nature.

AT HOME

AROUND TOWN

IN NATURE

At the beginning of each section, there is an infographic describing the **benefits** of spending time in each of the three kinds of environments.

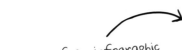

Example of an infographic about nature

There are so many activities we can enjoy with our families in each environment. The appropriate ages for each activity is clearly marked. **As Maria Montessori said, "Follow the children."** Whether we are at home, or in nature, or out and about downtown, we don't need screens to enjoy the company of the people we love.

Introduction

How do we enjoy free time with our family?

Routines form part of our every day life; waking up, getting dressed, washing our face, eating breakfast, going to school. Everyone has an unending to-do list and obligations that take up our time. But when we have "free time," do we know how to enjoy it? And more importantly, **do we know how to enjoy it with our family?**

Small moments during the week

Time with family is so important and is not limited just to relaxing moments and breaks from work on the weekend. Beyond Saturdays and Sundays, the week is full of small moments we can enjoy with family, even if sometimes they get lost in the hustle and bustle of everyday life.

A good way to begin to spend more time with your family is if the adults **organize time** during which you can use phones, tablets or other screens that take us out of the moment. This doesn't mean we can't use these things, but rather that we should be conscious of the world around us and **know how to enjoy the possibilities** that technology can present us with daily. In fact, if it weren't for technology, you might not be able to read this book.

Screens take us out of the moment

We aren't trying to be radical, but rather to just be present in what we are doing, saying, and feeling. **A few good tickles are worth more than a nice picture**. And even though it is important to have photos of important moments, it is just as important to enjoy some cuddles and laughter without a photo.

You can enjoy moments without documenting them

No one can deny that **screen time can also create family moments.** On the weekends, when we have a lot of family time, we often choose to watch a movie. It's very nice to snuggle up on the couch on a rainy day with a blanket, some popcorn, and the fireplace going. And this is not the only possible plan!

A cozy movie marathon

365 screen-free family activities

There is a life outside of screen time, even though it is sometimes hard to come up with activities to do with your family. This book is a guide that contains 365 screen-free family activities. Each activity is a **great tool** to begin an adventure, a little experiment, and to grow with everyone as a family.

And we can ask ourselves, how can an activity book do all of this? Because in this book, the activities are not the end, but only **the beginning of spending time with your family**. Each activity is a different idea with the same objective: **to strengthen bonds** and help pass the time in a way that helps you grow as a family. You will never have to ask "what do you want to do?" only to be met with crickets, and ending up back on your devices due to a lack of ideas.

The adventure begins here

Ready in a jiffy!

Here are activities to do as a family, activities that don't need a ton of materials or a lot of preparation. Time is often not on our side, but in Screen-Free Family Activities, the main ingredient is the enthusiasm to **share this time with each other**. There are simple activities, and other more elaborate activities, including activities that only take five minutes to do. It is these minutes that are so important emotionally for children.

365 activities that invite you to **use your imagination, create connections, practice building and dreaming.** To realize that television, phones, and other screens aren't necessary. We only need our family to help us learn, experiment, and have fun together.

Activities that use your imagination, create connections, practice building and dreaming

ACTIVITIES: Being at Home with Family

1. The Mystery Box
2. Bubble Beards and Hairdos
3. Painting on the Windows
4. Art on Continuous Paper
5. Camping at Home
6. Pajama Party
7. Storytelling Night
8. Balloon Day
9. Family Handprint Painting
10. Picnic in the Living Room
11. Load the Washing Machine
12. Searching for Buried Treasure — *This is very fun*
13. **At-Home Spa**
14. Cushion Bridge
15. A Jar Full of Nice Words
16. Organizing the Coat Rack
17. Cookie and Snack
18. Toilet Paper Roll puppets
19. Battered Bananas
20. Carve a Pumpkin
21. Paint with Your Feet
22. Jumping on the Bed
23. Morning of Massages
24. Family Photos
25. Clean the House
26. **Volcano Experiment**
27. Belly-Laugh Workout
28. Cat's Cradle
29. Guess the Gesture
30. Arranging Flowers
31. Spider web
32. Paint a Shopping Bag
33. Volleyball
34. Pasta Necklace

35. Cleaning Spray
36. Send Postcards
37. Make Tickets
38. Soap Bubbles
39. Dance Party
40. Reciting Tongue-twisters, Poems, and Jokes
41. Hallway Obstacle Course
42. **Magic Show** — *Ta-da!*
43. Create a Domino Effect
44. Put on Makeup Blindfolded
45. Make a Swimming Pool in the Bathtub
46. Take a Bath in a Bucket — *Refreshing!*
47. The Robot
48. Walk Like Cats
49. Family Timeline
50. What is Missing?
51. Build a Cabin (Under the Dining Room Table)
52. Hide and Seek
53. Talent Show
54. Art Exposition
55. Grape Stomping
56. Hairdressing — *with crazy hairdos*
57. **Ice Cream Shop**
58. Fold the Laundry
59. Snuggle Break
60. Set the Table
61. Manicure Appointment
62. What Animal Am I?
63. Fruit Skewers — *Mmmm... delicious!*
64. Tattoo Shop — *Mother's Love*
65. Pillows
66. Stuffed Dates
67. Toy Factory
68. Homemade Pizza

You can mark off the activities you've completed ✓

- ○ **69.** Plan a Trip
- ○ **70.** Seasonal Basket
- ○ **71.** Stacking Toilet Paper
- ○ **72.** Mega-Construction
- ○ **73.** Create a Family Motto
- ○ **74.** Flower Shop
- ○ **75.** Taste Test
- ○ **76.** Make Apple Slice Donuts
- ○ **77.** Family Collage
- ○ **78.** Pirate Voyage
- ○ **79.** A Night at the Theater
- ○ **80.** Secret Message ← *Top Secret*
- ○ **81.** Time Capsule
- ○ **82.** Conversation Starters
- ○ **83.** Family Activity Jar
- ○ **84.** Mummies ← *guaranteed laughs*
- ○ **85.** Family Tree
- ○ **86.** Do the Dishes or Load the Dishwasher
- ○ **87.** Fishing in the Bathtub
- ○ **88.** Family Memory
- ○ **89.** Science Night
- ○ **90.** Gratitude Jar
- ○ **91.** Blowing a Ball
- ○ **92.** Play Restaurant
- ○ **93.** Making a Schedule
- ○ **94.** Home Delivery
- ○ **95.** Happy Teeth
- ○ **96. Family Meeting** ← *We are getting organized*
- ○ **97.** Recycling Center
- ○ **98.** Reusable Bags for the Pantry
- ○ **99.** Making Popcorn
- ○ **100.** Bobbing for Apples
- ○ **101.** The Quiet Game
- ○ **102.** Catching Oranges with Your Knees

- ○ **103.** Sensory Socks
- ○ **104.** Switching Roles
- ○ **105.** Listen to Music Lying Down
- ○ **106.** Sensory Walkway
- ○ **107.** Experiment with Oranges ← *Look! So Interesting!*
- ○ **108.** Painting with Shaving Cream
- ○ **109.** Walk in a Line
- ○ **110.** Alphabet Lids
- ○ **111.** What Feeling is on My Head?
- ○ **112.** Elephant Game
- ○ **113.** Fishing for Lids
- ○ **114.** Covered in Post-Its
- ○ **115.** Disco Night
- ○ **116.** Spoon Transfer
- ○ **117. Home Bookstore**
- ○ **118.** Match Socks ← *birds of a feather flock together*
- ○ **119.** Family Wall
- ○ **120.** Tea Party
- ○ **121.** Ice Painting
- ○ **122.** Veterinary Clinic
- ○ **123.** Bathing the Baby
- ○ **124.** Daily Chores
- ○ **125.** Frozen Fossils
- ○ **126.** Family Sticker Album
- ○ **127.** Self-Portrait
- ○ **128.** Apple Sandwiches ← *yummy*
- ○ **129.** Tightrope Walker
- ○ **130.** Paper Cup Tower
- ○ **131.** Draw Yourself in the Mirror
- ○ **132.** Wish Board
- ○ **133.** Sumo Cushions
- ○ **134.** Linear Calendar
- ○ **135.** Telephone Game
- ○ **136.** Human Knot

ACTIVITIES: Enjoying the City as a Family

- ○ 137. **City Kit**
- ○ 138. Observe an Anthill
- ○ 139. Types of Kisses (Eskimo, Butterfly, Cow)
- ○ 140. Feed the Pigeons
- ○ 141. Crosswalks
- ○ 142. Observing Snails
- ○ 143. Visit a Museum
- ○ 144. Visit a Library
- ○ 145. Train Adventure
- ○ 146. Go to a Musical *It's a musical!*
- ○ 147. Visit a Botanical Garden
- ○ 148. Visit a Farmers' Market
- ○ 149. Play in the Sprinklers
- ○ 150. **Reusing Napkins**
- ○ 151. Enjoying a Meal in a Restaurant
- ○ 152. Excursion on a Tourist Bus Around the City
- ○ 153. Play "I Spy"
- ○ 154. Chasing Pigeons
- ○ 155. Puddle Jumping *beep beep!*
- ○ 156. Skating
- ○ 157. Visit Family
- ○ 158. Visit a Climbing Wall
- ○ 159. Read the Signs You Find
- ○ 160. Visit a Senior Living Residence
- ○ 161. Go Out for Ice Cream
- ○ 162. Take an Urban Art Tour *works of art in the city*

- ○ 163. **Juggling**
- ○ 164. Rock, Paper, Scissors
- ○ 165. Attend a Play
- ○ 166. Visit a Flea Market
- ○ 167. Ride a Carousel *around and around*
- ○ 168. Have a Picnic in the Park
- ○ 169. Hidden Treasures
- ○ 170. Follow the Chain
- ○ 171. Donate Toys/Clothes/Food
- ○ 172. Go to a Concert
- ○ 173. Walk in a Train
- ○ 174. Share and Propose
- ○ 175. Go Shopping at the Supermarket
- ○ 176. **Cleaning the City** *We are the champions!*
- ○ 177. Red Light, Green Light
- ○ 178. Attend a Sports Game
- ○ 179. Folding Napkins
- ○ 180. Draw with Chalk in the Park
- ○ 181. Give Flowers to Passersby
- ○ 182. Visit an Animal Refuge
- ○ 183. **Jumping Rope**
- ○ 184. Visit a Ball Pit
- ○ 185. Eat at a Food Truck
- ○ 186. Visit an Amusement Park
- ○ 187. Visit a Medieval Village
- ○ 188. Make Water Balloons in the Fountain *Splash splash*

you can mark off which activities you've completed ✓

- ◯ **189.** See a Storyteller Show
- ◯ **190. Observing a Puddle**
- ◯ **191.** Leave Messages at Cultural Destinations
- ◯ **192.** Enjoy a Day at the Spa
- ◯ **193.** Go to the Public Pool
- ◯ **194.** Clean the Car
- ◯ **195.** Go to the Skate Park
- ◯ **196.** Have a Snack
- ◯ **197. Road Safety** ← *choo choo*
- ◯ **198.** Write and Send a Letter
- ◯ **199.** Crab Walk Game
- ◯ **200.** Hopscotch
- ◯ **201.** Take an Airplane
- ◯ **202.** Visit the "Forest" in the Bushes at the Park
- ◯ **203.** Identify the Trees in Your City
- ◯ **204. Handkerchief Game**
- ◯ **205.** Play Tag
- ◯ **206.** Collecting Leaves
- ◯ **207.** Search for Treasure in the Park
- ◯ **208.** Hand Clapping Games
- ◯ **209.** Guess the Feeling
- ◯ **210.** Visit Ruins ← *super interesting*
- ◯ **211. Facial Expressions in Magazines**
- ◯ **212.** Ride a Scooter
- ◯ **213.** See a Music Group
- ◯ **214.** Go to a Street Fair

there's a party in the street! ↗

- ◯ **215.** Help at a Soup Kitchen
- ◯ **216.** Word Chain
- ◯ **217.** Play Petanque
- ◯ **218. The Blind Hen**
- ◯ **219.** Wheelbarrow
- ◯ **220.** Visit a Riverbank
- ◯ **221.** Visit a Famous Monument
- ◯ **222.** Enjoy a Bike Ride
- ◯ **223.** Look at the City from the Tallest Building
- ◯ **224.** Create at a Craft Workshop
- ◯ **225. Draw Shadows** ← *What do you think will happen?*
- ◯ **226.** Stay on the Line
- ◯ **227.** Origami
- ◯ **228.** Go to a Yoga Class ← *Ommmm... Shanti Shanti*
- ◯ **229.** Sidewalk Maze
- ◯ **230.** Phrases with Vowels
- ◯ **231.** Pack a Suitcase
- ◯ **232. Cat and Mouse**
- ◯ **233.** Take a Ferry
- ◯ **234.** Visit a Traditional Oven
- ◯ **235.** Jump on a Trampoline
- ◯ **236.** Ride on a Cable Car
- ◯ **237.** The Mirror (Copy Me!)

Good for practicing symmetry ↖

ACTIVITIES: Enjoying Nature as a Family

238. **Nature Kit**
239. Find Almonds in Bloom
240. Pick Flowers
241. Sand Tray
242. Measure the Width of a Tree
243. Counting the Rings in a Tree Trunk
244. Plant a Fruit Tree
245. Run Along the Beach
246. Pick Chestnuts
247. Bark Rubbing
248. Catch a Bug to Observe
249. Dreamcatchers
250. Observe Seashells
251. Get Muddy
252. Plant a Tree
253. Roll on the Grass
254. Make a Snow Cake
255. Make a Tree Fort
256. Hug a Tree
257. Nighttime Excursion to See the Stars
258. Clean the Beach or Forest
259. Drawing in the Sand
260. Make a Wish on a Dandelion
261. Storytelling on Rocks
262. **How a Plant Breathes**
263. Natural Candle
264. What Are You Touching?
265. Bury Your Feet in the Sand
266. Go Sledding
267. Make a Wreath of Leaves
268. Observe Rocks
269. Create a Sensory Walk
270. Have a Picnic

271. Make a Snow Man
272. Visit a Nature Reserve
273. Paint in the Snow
274. Visit a Farm
275. **Natural Feather Dusters**
276. Make an Air Freshener with Oranges and Cloves
277. Is it Windy?
278. Homemade Soap
279. Muddy Rainy Days
280. Yarn Sticks
281. Pinecone Hedgehogs
282. Breathe, Reconnect
283. Natural Textures
284. Building a Sand Castle
285. Weaving with Natural Objects
286. Hiking Route
287. Sleep Under the Stars
288. **God's Eye**
289. Fireside Storytelling
290. Paintbrushes with Sticks + Natural Elements
291. Drawing Faces on Leaves
292. Find a Tree
293. Make Numbers on Rocks
294. Insect Refuge
295. Watch the Sunset
296. Mud Dolls
297. Flower Petal Garlands
298. Bending Water
299. See the Sunrise
300. Natural Colors
301. **Biodegradation**
302. Observing Tadpoles in a Puddle
303. Enjoy a Rainbow
304. Observing Spiderwebs

¡Qué bien huele!

Remember the raincoat!

Help the planet

Old-fashioned painting

How cool!

Look for a high place

This is why they're colored!

You can check off when you've completed the activities

○ 305. Tracing the Shadow of a Tree

○ 306. Make a Mud Painting

○ 307. Make Lavender Perfume

○ 308. Use a Tree as an Easel

309. Make a Solar Clock

○ 310. Play with Water Toys in a Puddle

○ 311. Decorate Feathers with Beads

312. Look for the First Signs of Spring

○ 313. Draw on a Mirror in Nature

○ 314. **Chlorophyll** Experiment

Green with envy

○ 315. Shapes and Plates

○ 316. Climb a Bale of Hay

○ 317. Leaf Skewers

○ 318. Balancing on Tree Trunks

○ 319. Keep an Apple from Oxidizing

○ 320. Color a Picture and Leave It in the Rain

○ 321. Ice Cream Sundaes with Dirt, Flowers + Leaves

○ 322. Mystery Bag

○ 323. Sensory Bottles

○ 324. Potpourri Bags

○ 325. Singing in the Rain

○ 326. Dehydrate Fruit

○ 327. **Make a Bird Feeder**

○ 328. Orange Peel Candle Holder

○ 329. Mud Cakes

○ 330. Measure Rain with a Cup

○ 331. Water the Garden

○ 332. Grow Seasonal Fruits and Vegetables

○ 333. Harvest Your Garden

○ 334. Collect Treasures from Nature in an Egg Carton

○ 335. Find Objects in Nature that Match in Color

○ 336. Citrus Necklace

○ 337. Object Search Game

○ 338. Jump in the Leaves

Autumn arrives, red and yellow

○ 339. Nature Collage

○ 340. **Wash Apples**

○ 341. Tic-Tac-Toe in Nature

○ 342. Nature Mobile

○ 343. Ice Wreath

○ 344. Go Camping

the water is nice!

○ 345. Swim in a River

○ 346. Planets Orbiting the Sun

○ 347. Grow a Seed

○ 348. Find a Cicada Shell

Changing their outfit

○ 349. Ride a Tractor

○ 350. Skipping Stones

○ 351. Cartwheels in a Meadow

○ 352. Collect Sunflower Seeds

○ 353. **Recycle Paper**

○ 354. Puddles at the Beach

○ 355. Take a Walk in a Grove

○ 356. Popcorn Garlands for the Birds

○ 357. Visit a Bird Observatory

○ 358. Dress a Tree

○ 359. Ride in a Canoe

The Earth spins around the sun

○ 360. Celebrate Earth Day

○ 361. Walk in a Cornfield

○ 362. Observe Fish

○ 363. Climb Rocks

○ 364. Collect Mountain Plants

○ 365. Walnut Shell Necklaces

BENEFITS OF
Being at Home with Family

1 LEARNING FROM YOUR MISTAKES

It is important to understand that mistakes are part of the learning process, even for adults. Family can provide this opportunity to learn.

2 COOPERATE AND SHARE

To create a healthy functioning household, everyone must understand that it is important to collaborate and share in work, solutions, and activities. Sharing can be fun!

3 RESPONSIBILITY

Chores and other household activities can demonstrate the value of responsibility.

4 ORGANIZATION

Creating an organized environment doesn't mean things always need to be perfect, but rather that we need to be respectful of other family members and understand that our actions affect others. Systems of organization help everyone agree on how to keep things organized.

5 PATIENCE

Things don't stay the same from day to day, and it is important to keep in mind that "we learn from our mistakes" and nobody is perfect. To make mistakes is a gift in life to help us learn. Patience is the support that sustains a family.

6 RESPECT

It is essential to respect all members of the family. Every person is learning in one way or another, and above all, we need to treat others with respect.

① Mystery Box

❄ ❀ ☀ 🍁 2+ years

🕐 15 minutes

Find a cardboard box. Cut two holes for your hands in one side. Leave the other side open. One person will put their hands through the holes, while the other person will find objects to put in the open side. The object of the game is to guess what objects you are touching.

② Bubble Beards and Hairdos

❄ ❀ ☀ 🍁 12+ months

🕐 20 minutes

You can create special memories during bathtime. All you need is a bathtub and some no-tears soap. While you are taking a bath, create some bubbles and you can make mustaches, beards, glasses, and hair from the foam!

③ Painting on the Windows

❄ ❀ ☀ 🍁 14+ months

🕐 15 minutes

Draw the moon, a name, or a tree. You can draw whatever you want on the glass. Using special erasable felt markers and your artistic spirit, you can experiment on this canvas, which provides a different texture than the paper you are used to. It can be fun for the family to create a collaborative piece of art.

④ Art on Continuous Paper

❄ ✿ ☀ 🍁 **12+ months**

🕐 15 minutes

Paints, hands, feet, and a roll of paper. The possibilities are endless. You can draw any story you can imagine!

For very young children, you can mix yogurt with food coloring. They can paint on the paper, and you don't have to worry about them eating it!

⑤ Camping at Home

❄ ✿ ☀ 🍁 **2+ years**

🕐 20 minutes

No time to travel? No worries! There is always room in the living room, no matter how small, to set up a tent (just like what we use when we're camping without having to nail anything into the ground). Create an unforgettable and authentic experience with a "cave" to hide in, to dream in, and to tell stories by flashlight.

⑥ Pajama Party

❄ ✿ ☀ 🍁 **2+ years**

🕐 20 minutes

Fun has come right to your home! It's time to put on your pajamas. You can make a dinner of finger foods, snuggle up with blankets and cushions, play a little music, and have fun!

⑦ Storytelling Night

❄ ✿ ☀ 🍁 **12+ months**

🕐 20 minutes

Something fun to do as a family is to tell stories: a warm blanket and a pile of stories, one after the other, in a pillow fort, on the couch or in bed. Any place is a good place to read and dream!

⑧ Balloon Day

❄ ✿ ☀ 🍁 **2+ years**

🕐 20 minutes

Can you imagine a house filled from floor to ceiling with balloons of all colors? You will need lots of balloons. Fill them up yourself or with a pump, and let them go! Fill every corner with balloons!

⑨ Family Handprint Painting

❄ ✿ ☀ 🍁 **12+ months**

🕐 20 minutes

One of the most entertaining things you can do is make a painting with your hands. On one sheet, you can take every family member's handprints and keep them forever. You can do one every year and see how they grow and change.

You don't have to stop with handprints! You can draw trees, chickens, a train and all its passengers. Or whatever you want!

10 Picnic in the Living Room

❄ ✿ ☀ 🍁 2+ years

🕐 20 minutes

What do you do when the weather outside is bad? No problem! Find a blanket and a basket! A picnic on the floor of the house is always a good plan: snacks, fruit, dried fruits, chips, drinks, and everything is ready for you to enjoy this family moment! You don't have to go far to create unforgettable moments.

11 Load the Washing Machine

❄ ✿ ☀ 🍁 12+ months

🕐 10 minutes

Our babies love to explore, discover, investigate, and learn every single day. Every day, they develop more and more autonomy. Because of this, something as simple as filling the washing machine is an ideal activity for the whole family. What's more, it can include family members of all ages, each with their own task: to sort the clothes, load the machine, pour the soap, and turn it on. Working as a team is always a good option!

12 Searching for Buried Treasure

❄ ✿ ☀ 🍁 2+ years

🕐 20 minutes

A precious object hidden away, a map of the house, and different clues can create a fun adventure without leaving the house.

Treasure map templates are available online.

At-Home Spa

 2+ years

🕐 1 hour

It is time to relax!

You don't have to go to exotic places to combine fun and relaxation into the perfect plan. You can work wonders with the right materials right at home! Surely you already have more than half of the materials!

It is important to choose a peaceful place to do this activity. The priority is to focus on your family.

Then all you need is to set the scene as if you were in a real spa.

A great routine can begin with your feet in a tub of hot or cold water, depending on the time of year, or with one after the other in order to create a contrast in temperature. You can continue with massages with oil, on the sofa or bed, and follow by putting on lotion, a face mask, or whatever other things you like. Finally, you can sit quietly to relax in peace.

MATERIALS

- Bucket
- Hand towel
- Bathrobe
- Towel for your feet
- Lotions and oils
- Massage roller
- Opaque eye mask
- Nail polish
- Seats or cushions for each family member
- Bed/couch and a towel/sheet to protect it

DID YOU KNOW?

In Rome, Greece, and Egypt, people used thermal baths, scented creams, and massages. But not everyone had the same access or privilege in these cultures, and these luxuries were reserved for only the wealthiest people to treat their bodies.

(14) Cushion Bridge

❄ ✿ ☀ 🍁 3+ years

🕐 15 minutes

Let's make a path with pillows! If you have two couches, you can make it go from couch to couch to create a bridge to travel between them. The idea is to walk on top of the pillows, carefully, so as not to fall, as if the cushions were surrounded by water. You can imagine you are crossing a bridge surrounded by danger or taking a walk through the clouds.

(15) A Jar Full of Nice Words

❄ ✿ ☀ 🍁 4+ years

🕐 20 minutes

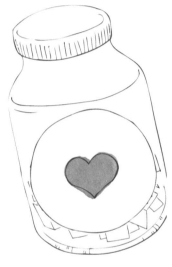

Decorate a jar, a jam jar for example, and use it to collect words you write down. You can add these words to the jar any day, at any time. You can write down words you find interesting or funny, or perhaps you simply like how they sound. When the jar is full, you can play a game taking words out, reading them aloud, and seeing how they make you feel.

You can find stickers and drawings for your jar online, or on our website. See note on page 4.

(16) Organizing the Coatrack

❄ ✿ ☀ 🍁 18+ months

🕐 25 minutes

Organize your coatrack by decorating it with words or illustrations to help show where items go. Arrange items so that they are easy to find and take on and off the rack. It is important to remember to organize items while considering the height of different family members, putting the tallest member's items at the top and shorter members at the bottom.

You can find stickers and drawings for your coatrack online, or on our website. See note on page 4.

17 Cookie and Snack

❄ ✿ ☀ 🍁 4+ years

🕐 5 minutes

Take a cookie and try to hold it in your eye, letting it slide little by little down your face until it reaches your mouth so you can eat it. Don't let it fall! Warning: Laughter is guaranteed and will definitely make this operation more difficult.

18 Toilet Paper Roll Puppets

❄ ✿ ☀ 🍁 4+ years

🕐 20 minutes

Who said toilet paper rolls only belong in the bathroom? Here is an ingenious use for them! Eyes, mouth, hair, clothes, you can decorate these rolls however you like! Now the show begins!

19 Battered Bananas

❄ ✿ ☀ 🍁 2+ years

🕐 10 minutes

This is an extra sweet activity. Cut a banana in half, then put it on a popsicle stick, lollipop stick, or skewer, and dip it in your choice of spread (peanut butter, cashew butter, sunflower butter, etc.) or chocolate. Then you can dip them in oats, chopped nuts (dried fruits advisable for 5 years and up), raisins, or whatever else you like and they're ready to eat!

(20) Carve a Pumpkin

🍁 **2+ years**

🕐 20 minutes

You will need one pumpkin per person. First cut open the top and then use a spoon to scoop out the insides. The seeds can be roasted and eaten as a snack, while the pulp is delicious sautéed, baked, or made into a purée or marmalade. Now that your pumpkin is empty, you can carve a face or a design and put a candle inside to make a jack-o'-lantern. There are endless possibilities!

(21) Paint with Your Feet

❄️ ❀ ☀ 🍁 **2+ years**

🕐 20 minutes

Find a receptacle that is shallow and sturdy to hold the finger paint. Cover the floor well, and unroll your roll of paper. Now, dip your feet in the paint and walk all over the paper, slowly, making footprints with the bottoms and sides of your feet. Pay attention to how the prints change depending on the position of the feet. Have a tub of water ready to help clean your feet and a towel for drying. You can choose the section you like the best to hang in your house as a work of art. You can have more than one favorite!

(22) Jumping on the Bed

❄️ ❀ ☀ 🍁 **18+ months**

🕐 5 minutes

This is a great way to release some energy, have some laughs, and create some family fun! We grow up so fast and so rarely get to jump on the bed!

(23) Morning of Massages

❄ 🌸 ☀ 🍁 **4+ years**

🕐 5 minutes

Oils, scented lotions, rollers, feathers, clothes. Let's take turns giving massages! Create a relaxing ambiance and give massages for whatever body part you choose. If you like, tickles are allowed!

(24) Family Photos

❄ 🌸 ☀ 🍁 **12+ months**

🕐 15–20 minutes

Remembering our past is an important part of our story. Who is this man with the glasses? Why is Grandma wearing her hair like this? Where is this? What were we doing? Where did we travel and how did we get there? Looking at family photos is a perfect excuse to remember moments and laugh, cry, hug, and get to know each other a little better.

(25) Clean the House

❄ 🌸 ☀ 🍁 **18+ months**

🕐 10–20 minutes

Every person in the family can clean one area of the house. One can sweep, others can dust, another can straighten up. And of course, you can play fun music to get you moving and make the activity more fun!

(26) Volcano Experiment

❄ ❀ ☀ 🍁 **2+ years**

🕐 30 minutes

You don't have to travel around the world to see a volcano. And this is no ordinary volcano—it's a volcano in your own home! And you can make it with items you already have in the house.

First, you knead the modeling clay and use it to create the body of the volcano on a sheet pan, leaving a cavity at the top where the chimney will be and where the lava will come out.

When you're ready, make the magma chamber. Then put baking soda in a coffee mug and, if you want, add red food coloring to make the lava red, and detergent to create some foam, and pour this into the cavity.

Finally, pour in a trickle of vinegar and—*Boom!* The volcano erupts!

MATERIALS

- Brown and orange or red modeling clay
- Baking soda
- Red food coloring
- Apple cider vinegar
- Warm water and soap for handwashing

DID YOU KNOW?

The soil left after a volcano erupts is very fertile. If you farm in this soil, you will have great results, even after a long time. However, you may not want to live close to an active volcano.

(27) Belly-Laugh Workout

❄️ 🌼 ☀️ 🍁 4+ years

🕐 15 minutes

For this game, you will be seated on the floor, but in a specific way: it is important to form a train with all the seated people. Once you're seated in a line, each person will rest their head on the belly of the person behind them. Next, the first person in the line will make a big laugh, saying "HA!" forcefully! (So loud someone can hear it all the way in New Zealand!) The next person will make two laughs: "HA! HA!" The third person will make three laughs: "HA! HA! HA!" and so on until the last person. This should bounce everyone's heads up from the bellies they're resting on. Who said exercise can't be fun?!

(28) Cat's Cradle

❄️ 🌼 ☀️ 🍁 5+ years

🕐 5 minutes

For this activity, you will need a long string about 3 feet (1 meter) in length. You can play in pairs or take turns. To begin, make a knot in the string tying the ends together and wrap it around your hands, creating a figure with your fingers. Once the shape has been made, the next person will observe the shape and take it from their hands and make a new shape. You can make as many shapes and figures as you want!

DID YOU KNOW?

Cat's Cradle is a traditional game known around the world, from Japan to Hawaii to France. It is considered art in some cultures.

(29) Guess the Gesture

❄️ 🌼 ☀️ 🍁 5+ years

🕐 30 minutes

In this family game, you will have to use all your effort. Take turns whispering into another player's ear the name of something you like: a favorite dish, book, song, or location, for example. The next person, once they've heard what you whispered, has to try to communicate to the other players what you said using only gestures. Keep changing roles until everyone has had a chance to play. It is a fun way to get to know each other better!

(30) Arranging Flowers

❄ ✿ ☀ 🍁 **18+ months**

🕐 15–20 minutes

Pick some flowers from around your neighborhood or in the woods and bring them home. Prepare some small vases with a little water, and get some scissors, a funnel, and a tablecloth.

Each family member can choose a vase and cut the flowers they like the best and create a flower arrangement to decorate the house. Use the funnel to add water to each vase.

(31) Spider Web

❄ ✿ ☀ 🍁 **4+ years**

🕐 20–30 minutes

For this activity, all you need is a hoop—the bigger it is, the easier this activity will be—tape and toilet paper. Use the tape to make a spider web inside the hoop. Hang the hoop in a doorway and make balls with the toilet paper. Take turns throwing balls at the tape web, trying to get them to stick. Count how many balls the family is able to get to stick to the web.

(32) Paint a Shopping Bag

❄ ✿ ☀ 🍁 **4+ years**

🕐 5 minutes

Paint or fabric markers can give new life to an old tote bag. Everyone can choose the colors they like to create their artwork before they paint! Now you can go shopping with a unique and original shopping bag.

(33) Volleyball

❄ ✿ ☀ 🍁 **4+ Years**

🕐 20 minutes

For this volleyball match, you will need to construct a net. You can tie a sheet between two posts. Blow up a balloon and pass it from side to side over the net. Make sure the balloon doesn't touch the floor!

(34) Pasta Necklace

❄ ✿ ☀ 🍁 **2+ years**

🕐 20 minutes

Choose a pasta shape that is easy to thread with a string. You can dye the pasta using water and food coloring, leaving the pasta in the water for a few minutes, or hours to make the necklace even more beautiful. Then all you need to do is dry the pasta and you can create necklaces by putting string through the pieces.

(35) Cleaning Spray

❄ ✿ ☀ 🍁 **2+ years**

🕐 15 minutes

You will need: 1 cup of distilled water, 1 cup of vinegar, 20 drops of lemon essential oil, and 20 drops of tea tree essential oil.

Mix and pretend it is a magic potion, then pour into a spray bottle to clean the furniture.

(36) Send Postcards

❄ ✿ ☀ 🍁 **2+ years**

🕐 20 minutes

Gather your materials: card stock, markers, glue sticks, stickers, watercolors, scissors, and anything else you think would make a nice postcard. You don't need an occasion to create and send postcards. Anyone would want to receive a nice surprise! Spread out all your materials on the table and let the creativity flow!

You can find ready-made stickers and stencils online or on our website. See note on page 4.

(37) Make Tickets

❄ ✿ ☀ 🍁

🕐 15 minutes

Get some sheets of colored paper and cut them into shapes to draw on. You can make tickets, coins, and dollar bills and use them in any game that needs pretend currency.

You can find some pre-drawn tickets on our website. See note on page 4.

(38) Soap Bubbles

❄ ✿ ☀ 🍁 **12+ months**

🕐 5–15 minutes

You will need a bubble wand for every member of the family. This way you can take turns blowing bubbles, or getting to chase, catch, and pop them, observing them while they float until they burst. Or you can all blow a ton of bubbles at once!

(39) Dance Party

❄ ✿ ☀ 🍁 **12+ months**

🕐 20 minutes

Setting the scene for this activity is crucial: lights, streamers, balloons, everything you can think of to decorate the house like it's a party. Every person in the family can choose what songs or bands they want to hear and make a playlist, or you can take turns playing DJ and picking the songs.

(40) Reciting Tongue-twisters, Poems, and Jokes

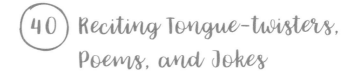

❄ ✿ ☀ 🍁 **6+ Years**

🕐 30 minutes

Each member of the family can take turns reciting a poem, tongue-twister, or joke. If you want to make it a little more challenging, try holding a spoon in your mouth with a small ball balanced on the end of it. Recite your piece without dropping the spoon or the ball—and make sure not to laugh!

(41) Hallway Obstacle Course

❄ ✿ ☀ 🍁 **2+ years**

🕐 25 minutes

For this activity, you need a clear hallway. Use tape, string, or rope to create zigzagging lines from one wall to the other, all the way down. Try to get down the hallway without touching any of the strings or getting stuck on the tape!

(42) Magic Show

❄ ❁ ☀ 🍁 **2+ years**

🕐 15–20 minutes

Abracadabra! Who doesn't love a good show? Magic brings joy to people of all ages, especially very young children who are excited to join in every game. It is always a good day for a magic trick, to put on a top hat, to make objects appear and disappear, and to enjoy a surprise.

Preparation is important. Choose your outfit, decide who will host the show and which tricks to perform.

DID YOU KNOW?

René Lavand was an illusionist who only had one hand. He specialized in card tricks, performing illusions all over the world with his famous phrase, "It cannot be done any slower."

MATERIALS

- Magic tricks
- Top hat
- Stage area

"If you believe it, it exists."

Antonio Navarro

TA-DA!

43) Create a Domino Effect

❄ ✿ ☀ 🍁 **4+ years**
🕐 15–20 minutes

For this activity, you will need some pieces of wood. Set them up in a long line on the floor. The more pieces you have, the more interesting the activity will be. Is it possible to create a domino effect that stretches the entire length of the house? That would be incredible!

44) Put on Makeup Blindfolded

❄ ✿ ☀ 🍁 **18+ months**
🕐 15 minutes

This will be a unique experience! It's important to gather all the makeup together in a basket or on a table so the person who is applying the makeup blindfolded can find everything easily. Let everyone choose if they want to be the one applying the makeup or getting the makeover. The best part is looking in the mirror to see the final result!

45) Make a Swimming Pool in the Bathtub

❄ ✿ ☀ 🍁 **3+ years**
🕐 15 minutes

Going to the pool is always a fun plan. To put a fun twist on it, pretend your bathtub is a swimming pool and put on your bathing suit and swimming cap. It isn't necessary to go as deep as you would in a swimming pool, but it is a good way to have some fun splashing around and laughing.

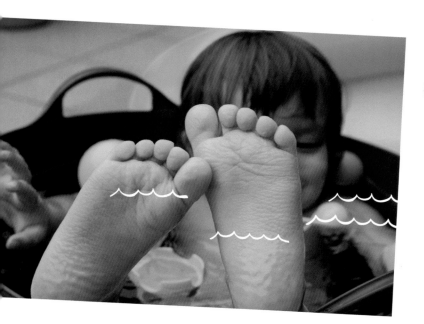

46) Take a Bath in a Bucket

☀ **18+ months**
🕐 15 minutes

This activity is best done outdoors, if you have a yard or a patio, so you don't have to worry about splashing water everywhere. The challenge will be seeing if any grownup can fit into the bucket. You can guess where all the water will go! Have fun!

(47) The Robot

❄ ✿ ☼ 🍁 **2+ years**

🕐 5 minutes

Position yourselves like this: the child will stand on top of the adult's feet, and the adult's arms will serve as the arms of the robot. The adult can walk like-a-ro-bot, with the child riding on top of their feet!

(48) Walk Like Cats

❄ ✿ ☼ 🍁 **8+ months**

🕐 15 minutes

Even though this activity seems most fitting for babies, it is a great way to see the world from the perspective of our littlest children. The whole family can walk around the house on all fours like a cat, examining every inch from this new perspective.

(49) Family Timeline

❄ ✿ ☼ 🍁 **5+ years**

🕐 25 minutes

It's time to remember!

Use a piece of paper to create a family timeline. How did the adults in the family meet? When? When were you born? Where? When did you begin to walk? Record all of the important dates in your family. You can illustrate the events, or add a phrase or anecdote for each moment. You can frame your work when it's done. And you can make a timeline for each member of the family.

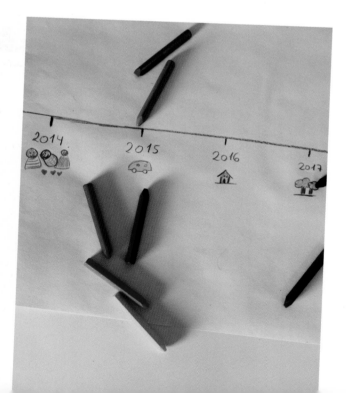

↘ **DID YOU KNOW?**

You store more memories in your head in a single day of vacation than in a whole week of normal routines.

(50) What is Missing?

❄️ 🌼 ☀️ 🍁 4–5+ years
🕐 30 minutes

Choose one member of the family to leave the room (you can take turns). Once they're gone, the other people will hide one object. Bring the person back into the room and let them guess which object is missing.

(51) Build a Cabin (Under the Dining Room Table)

❄️ 🌼 ☀️ 🍁 2+ months
🕐 15 minutes

A cabin doesn't have to be made of wood, and it doesn't have to be in the middle of the woods. If you have a dining room or kitchen table, cover it with a large sheet so the sides go all the way to the ground. Now you have a place to hide, play, or nap!

(52) Hide and Seek

❄️ 🌼 ☀️ 🍁 12+ months
🕐 15 minutes

This game is a must! One person closes their eyes and counts to 100 while the rest of the people hide: in the closets, under the beds, behind the doors. Who is the best at hiding? You will see!

(53) Talent Show

❄️ 🌼 ☀️ 🍁 2+ years
🕐 30 minutes

Everyone has a talent, something special they can do well. Tape off a stage area, pick an object (a pencil, a flip-flop, whatever you can find) to represent a microphone. All you need is a band and a host to introduce the acts, and you're ready to show off your singing, dancing, reciting, acting, and juggling!

(54) Art Exposition

❄ ✿ ☀ 🍂 2+ years

🕐 20 minutes

Find some room in the house to collect all the artwork you and your family members have made, from paintings to sculptures. Hang the paper pieces with frames, string, or on a display. For the sculptures, you can make a little shelf where you can collect them as you make them. Display your art!

(55) Grape Stomping

❄ ✿ ☀ 🍂 18+ months

🕐 15 minutes

You will need a bucket and a lot of grapes. Put the grapes in a bucket, take off your shoes, wash your feet well with soap and water, and begin to dance! Crush all the grapes till they make juice!

(56) Hairdressing

❄ ✿ ☀ 🍂 2+ years

🕐 10 minutes

Let your hair down!

This activity may sound scary, imagining our children cutting hair, but no! You don't have to risk your hair for this activity. You will be using dummy heads for this activity. Yes, dummies! You can get a dummy head for each family member to design their hairstyle. You will need scissors, scrunchies, headbands, and pins to create your unique hairstyles.

(57) Ice Cream Shop

✵ ✤ ☼ 🍁 **4+ years**

🕐 20 minutes

Ice cream, ice cream!

Who doesn't love ice cream? There's a flavor for everyone, even some of the most unusual flavors! This activity will certainly make everyone happy.

Use your table as the counter and find some different colored clay to make the "ice cream." You can create your own ice cream flavors and names, like "cloud-flavored ice cream" or "flower-flavored ice cream." Create a price for each flavor: one coin for vanilla and two to add sprinkles?

You can find materials for your ice cream shop on our website. See note on page 4.

MATERIALS

- Clay in different colors
- Ice cream scoop
- Paper cones
- Small spoons
- Printed tickets
- Name tags for the ice cream flavors
- Apron

DID YOU KNOW?

Ice cream is always being reinvented. Any food you can think of can be turned into an ice cream flavor. Fish, spaghetti, corn, the possibilities are endless. Would you try any of these?

58 Fold the Laundry

❄ ✿ ☀ 🍁 **3+ years**

🕐 20 minutes

Take your clean clothes and find a place where you can fold laundry. Let's get to work! Fold the clothes and put them away in their proper place.

59 Snuggle Break

❄ ✿ ☀ 🍁 **0+ months**

🕐 5 minutes

A cozy moment, a nice hug, some gentle words. And for older kids and teenagers, take a moment on the couch for some smiles, hugs, and interesting conversations.

60 Set the Table

❄ ✿ ☀ 🍁 **18+ months**

🕐 5 minutes

Glasses, napkins, plates, silverware and everything is ready for the family! Everyone can set the table! Take your favorite song and rewrite it, creating your own version about what you're doing. Everyone will come to dinner in a good mood!

You can find printable placemats online or on our website. See note on page 4.

61 Manicure Appointment

❄ ✿ ☀ 🍁 2+ years
🕐 10 minutes

Let's get to work!

Mom, Dad, Grandma, Grandpa, aunts and uncles are all invited to a family manicure appointment. Remember, nail polish remover and a towel are your friends.

62 What animal am I?

❄ ✿ ☀ 🍁 2+ years
🕐 5 minutes

Can you make the sound of a pig? Or a dog? Or maybe a tiger? Take turns guessing which animals you're acting out by the sound you're making!

WOOF
WOOF

63 Fruit Skewers

❄ ✿ ☀ 🍁 14+ months
🕐 15 minutes

There is no simpler recipe in the whole world! You will need skewers, cut fruit, and that is all you need to make your fruit skewers! (Remember to cut the fruit into age-appropriate bites.)

Mmmmm...

YUM

64 Tattoo Shop

 2+ years

🕐 15 minutes

Set up a table and make a sign advertising your tattoo shop. Gather the following materials: temporary tattoos, a spray bottle with water, body paints, and a little brush. Now you're ready to cover your body with drawings!

65 Pillows

 3+ years

🕐 15 minutes

Who hasn't had a pillow fight? Don't hit too hard, though! You can have fun just trying to bop each other with pillows or trying to crash the pillows together! The laughs are guaranteed!

67 Toy Factory

 4+ years

🕐 15 minutes

Can you imagine creating your own toy? It's possible! You will need string, wood blocks in all shapes and sizes, pom-poms, colored paper, tweezers, cones, sticks, and whatever else you think of. Put this all out on the table with room for the whole family. Use your imagination and create your own toys.

66 Stuffed Dates

 4–5+ years

🕐 20 minutes

Dates, peanut butter, almonds, and chocolate. You can use these ingredients to make a delicious, fast, and easy snack. Open the date and remove the pit. Fill with peanut butter, and if you want, you can put a little bit of dried fruit inside the date. Close up the date, and dip in melted chocolate. Get ready to lick your fingers!

If you want to make this treat a little less sweet, you can use cream cheese instead of the peanut butter and skip the chocolate dipping.

68) Homemade Pizza

❄️ 🌼 ☀️ 🍁 **14+ months**

🕐 20 minutes

What is better than a delicious pizza? And one made by the whole family, no less! The result is amazing! Invent your own pizza with the toppings you like best, and you can even make one half with one topping and the other half with another. The important thing is that everyone participates. The secret trick is to roll the dough out with a rolling pin. If you have a little extra dough, you can make mustaches, a nose, or whatever else you think is fun. Kids can draw each ingredient to help them follow the steps.

69) Plan a Trip

❄️ 🌼 ☀️ 🍁 **5+ years**

🕐 30 minutes

Where would you like to travel as a family? Unfold a big map onto the table and mark the places each family member wants to go. You can look for clippings, drawings, pictures, or journals from people who have been there. Each family member can explain why they want to travel there. Choose where you'd most want to go together as a family and begin to plan a trip.

70) Seasonal Basket

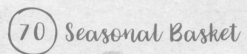

❄️ 🌼 ☀️ 🍁 **2+ years**

🕐 20 minutes

Dedicating a small space in your house to seasonal decorations can be very enriching for children, especially if you go out into nature to find objects that represent the season, such as flowers, nuts, leaves, etc.

You can make something like a flower arrangement dedicated to the time of year using these special objects. This is a great way to be aware of the season!

(71) Stacking Toilet Paper

❄️ 🌸 ☀️ 🍁 **12+ months**

🕐 10 minutes

Stacking toilet paper can be a family activity. You'll need a post on which you can drop the rolls of paper. Little children love stacking. If you don't have a post, no problem! You can organize the toilet paper in the bathroom.

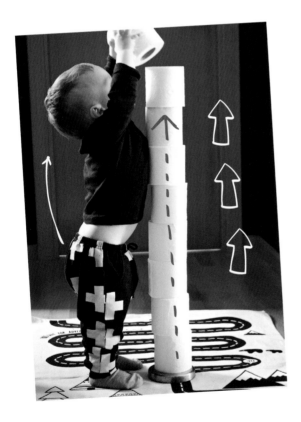

(72) Mega-Construction

❄️ 🌸 ☀️ 🍁 **2+ years**

🕐 15 minutes

What do you need? Lots of wood blocks! If you need more wood blocks, you can go to a carpenter to get some pieces and sand them. Use your blocks to build walls, and pretend you are in a palace or a tower. Try to make these structures touch the ceiling!

(73) Create a Family Motto

❄️ 🌸 ☀️ 🍁 **5+ years**

🕐 15 minutes

What is a family motto? Try to think of a commonly used phrase in your household. What do you want to remember every day? This is a motto. Family mottos can encourage and comfort us. Let's create something really special—a phrase that energizes us on a hard day!

You don't have to keep this motto for your whole life; you can change it every few months or yearly.

(74) Flower Shop

 3+ years

⏱ 15 minutes

The most important thing here is to set the scene so you can enjoy your activity to the max. In this case, try to create the environment of a flower shop: lots of green with plants, flowers, nice scents, and objects from nature. If you have one, set up a toy cash register. Once everything is ready, all you have to do is create bouquets or sell pots and planters. In this game, children will learn about numbers, money, and even bartering.

You can find materials for your flower shop online or on our website. See note on page 4.

(75) Taste Test

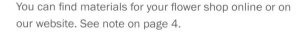 2+ years

⏱ 10 minutes

You will need a plate of different ingredients, and a blindfold or something to cover your eyes. Everyone can guess what foods they're eating and describe their flavors!

(76) Make Apple Slice Donuts

 2+ years

⏱ 15 minutes

Core and cut apples into rings. Put them on a plate and assemble the other ingredients: strawberries, peanut butter, melted chocolate, chocolate chips, and anything else you think of. Once you have everything together, spread peanut butter on each ring and decorate them with the rest of the ingredients. Now you have a delicious apple slice donut!

(77) Family Collage

❄️ ❀ ☀️ 🍁 **14+ months**

🕐 20 minutes

Art is a language that can take thoughts, feelings, concerns, and necessities and give them form. Family is a bit like art. For this reason, the possibility of capturing the essence of who you are is without a doubt something magical, especially if you do this as a team.

You will need magazines, newspapers, family photos, recycled materials, inspirational phrases, scissors, string, glue sticks, glitter, stickers, and homemade artwork. Have fun using your imagination and make a big collage to hang in the house—a collage that captures the energy and inspiration of each person in the family.

DID YOU KNOW?

Creating collages is used for therapeutic purposes. A collage can help us show our feelings that you otherwise might not be able to express.

(78) Pirate Voyage

❄️ ❀ ☀️ 🍁 **4+ years**

🕐 20 minutes

A map, a ship to sail on imaginary seas (the couch is perfect for this!), a mysterious place to explore, clues, and a fun costume (an eyepatch is essential!), and you will have an unforgettable pirate voyage!

(79) A Night at the Theater

❄️ ❀ ☀️ 🍁 **12+ months**

🕐 20 minutes

Make a big bowl of popcorn (to share with only those ages 4 years and up!), tickets, and everything you need to watch the show. Create the show you are going to watch. It can be a dance, a recital, puppets, whatever you want! You can enjoy this activity by taking turns: while one person eats popcorn, the others put on a show, and then you can switch.

(80) Secret Message

❄ ❀ ☀ 🍁 2+ years
🕐 5 minutes

Imagine you can communicate in a secret way that no one else can see. This is a secret message! How do you get ready? All you need is a candle, paper, and a crayon. Use the candle as a pencil and write (or draw) on the paper. Then your child can color the crayon over the whole paper. Bit by bit, they will reveal the message!

(81) Time Capsule

❄ ❀ ☀ 🍁 5+ years
🕐 20 minutes

A time capsule is a place where you can keep objects and current memories so that, at some point in the future, you can reflect back on this point in time.

You can make one with an empty cookie tin, a wooden box, or a lunchbox. To fill it, have each family member write a personal description, a funny story that happened this year, photos of important events, a special object, a newspaper article from this year, a playlist of your favorite current songs, and of course, a letter to your future self.

After the box is closed and sealed, hide it somewhere and choose a date to open it. How about in ten years? More? Will you be able to wait that long?

(82) Conversation Starters

❄ ❀ ☀ 🍁 6+ years
🕐 15 minutes

Think of the conversations you like to have with your family. Write these topics down on pieces of paper, or illustrate them with drawings, and put them in a bottle or jar. Use this bottle during family time to start conversations.

(83) Family Activity Jar

❄ ✿ ☀ 🍁 3+ years

🕐 1 hour

First, write each activity from this book on a piece of paper. Once you have all of them written out, cut them into their own pieces of paper. Since there are 365 ideas, every family member can have a turn writing, cutting, and helping.

Once they are all cut, put them inside a big jar so you can choose one every time you're stumped and can't think of what to do. The jar will always help you choose, and give you a surprise!

You can find stickers and drawings for your jar on our website. See note on page 4.

MATERIALS

- A document listing all the activities
- Jar
- Family photo
- Glue gun
- Scissors

DO YOU KNOW . . .?

Living with your family reduces the risk of developing depression.

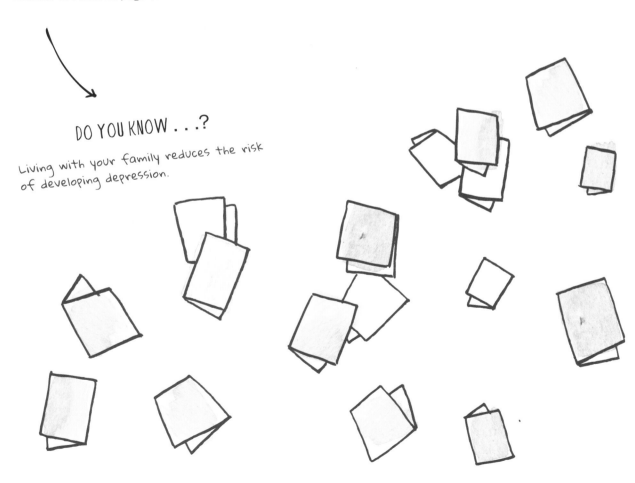

(84) Mummies

❄ ✿ ☀ 🍁 4+ years

🕐 10 minutes

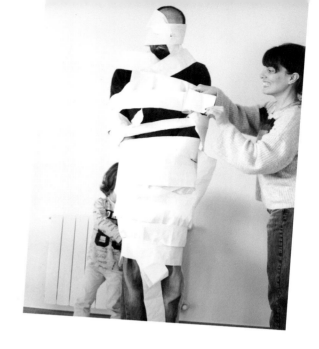

Do you dare to go back in time? There is nothing more fun than a costume, especially dressing up like a mummy! It is very simple. All you need is toilet paper and a good sense of humor. Take turns wrapping each family member. If you want to make it even more exciting, set a one-minute time limit for each person to finish wrapping. You will get so dizzy!

Remember to reuse your toilet paper for another activity!

(85) Family Tree

❄ ✿ ☀ 🍁 6+ years

🕐 20 minutes

For this activity, it's important to have or to take photos of every family member. Take a piece of paper and glue each photo to it corresponding to the correct branch of the tree, connecting them with lines. Next, under each photo, write a brief history or description of each person.

(86) Do the Dishes or Load the Dishwasher

❄ ✿ ☀ 🍁 2+ years

🕐 15 minutes

Water is calming, hydrating, and can be hypnotic for small children. Why not incorporate these properties into a family moment? Come on! Let's do the dishes! Enjoy the process, rather than the final result. This activity will be fun if you approach it with patience and humor!

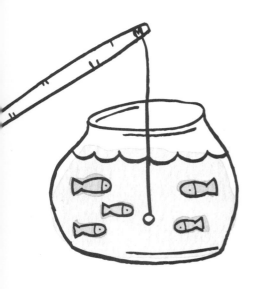

(87) Fishing in the Bathtub

❄ ❀ ☀ 🍂 2+ years

🕐 10 minutes

You will need ping pong balls, toys, Christmas ornaments, or rubber ducks. To fish, you'll need a net and a stick. Fill the bathtub with water and let the objects float on top. Go fishing for the objects and set a timer. See how many objects you can fish out in the set time!

(88) Family Memory

❄ ❀ ☀ 🍂 4+ years

🕐 20 minutes

Playing is essential, especially for young children, and *Memory* is a great game that is entertaining and educational. How good is your memory? You will need a picture of each family member, printed and laminated. Print each one twice to create a pair and go ahead and play!

(89) Science Night

❄ ❀ ☀ 🍂 4+ years

🕐 20 minutes

Turn your house into a laboratory! Prepare the craziest experiments you can think of. How about the volcano experiment from Activity 26? Or see what objects float and which ones sink? Maybe you can time how long it takes for an ice cube to melt on a plate? Does it take the same amount of time in a glass of water? Does the size of the ice cube impact the time it takes to melt? Your home is full of things that can make a fun experiment, but always be careful!

90 Gratitude Jar

❄ ✿ ☀ 🍂 **4+ years**

🕐 10 minutes

It's important to always remember what we are grateful for. One way to do this is to create a gratitude jar. This is a way to create a treasure for the whole family. You can also create individual jars for each person. Put a photo of the corresponding person on their jar.

These jars can be stored somewhere accessible so that you can always write and keep the things you are grateful for in the moment.

If you want, you can even do this alongside the family meeting, Activity 96.

You can find stickers and drawings for your jar online and on our website. See note on page TK.

DID YOU KNOW?

Expressing gratitude can increase happiness in both the person giving and the person receiving, and this is a gift that never expires or wears out.

91 Blowing a Ball

❄ ✿ ☀ 🍂 **4+ years**

🕐 15 minutes

You will need paper towel rolls, ping pong balls, a pair of paper cups, and some tape. Tape the paper cups to each end of the table and blow through the paper towel rolls to blow the ping pong balls into the cups.

92 Play Restaurant

❄ ✿ ☀ 🍂 **2+ years**

🕐 15 minutes

Assign some people to be the waiters and some to be the customers. This activity is great for practicing manners: "May I please have . . .?" "Thank you," "Could you be so kind as to . . .?" "Excuse me. . . ." This is also a fun way for the whole family to enjoy a meal together in a new way.

You can find some materials for your restaurant on our website. See note on page 4.

93 Making a Schedule

❄ ✿ ☀ 🍁 **18+ months**

🕐 20 minutes

Make a schedule for your daily activities, like going to school or work, taking a bath, reading a story, brushing your teeth, etc. Make a daily schedule for each person. You can tape these routines to the wall. This way you can know where each person is at any time of day.

You can find schedules and drawings on our website. See note on page 4.

94 Home Delivery

❄ ✿ ☀ 🍁 **4+ years**

🕐 15–25 minutes

This activity is really unique. Imagine you are placing an order with a restaurant and create two teams: one will be in the kitchen while the other is in the dining room. Create a menu with a list of ingredients that you can cook in the kitchen. Use walkie-talkies, or another way of communicating, like two clean and empty yogurt cups connected with a string, to communicate between the two teams.

One good idea is to make a pizza and draw the ingredients on the menu so each family member can choose the toppings for their pizza. Once they've decided, let the other team know the order and wait for them to make it. Two teams, one objective: eat!

95 Happy Teeth

❄ ✿ ☀ 🍁 **12+ months**

🕐 10 minutes

Brushing your teeth together is a good idea because it doesn't take much time and the whole family needs to do it. Let's brush our teeth! You can also play games making eye contact in the mirror and see who can keep from laughing the longest!

(96) Family Meeting

❄ ✿ ☀ ☘ 2+ years

🕐 20 minutes

The craziness of daily life can get in the way of spending time together, so a family meeting can be a great opportunity to create space for communication and understanding.

These meetings are, first and foremost, a moment to share with the family, to learn how to communicate, practice manners, learn what is important to other people. It is also an opportunity to learn how to create priorities, solve problems, and propose activities in a respectful way.

You can do this every week, or when there is something specific to resolve. Each family can decide for themselves. At first it can seem strange or complicated, but each time, you'll learn more about how to do this better. You can even keep a notebook to write down all the important parts.

These topics are ideas you can try at your family meeting:

1. GRATITUDE. One way to begin a meeting is to go around and say one thing each person is grateful for that week.

2. MATTERS TO DISCUSS AND POSSIBLE SOLUTIONS. You can come together to figure out anything that concerned you this week. Each person can think of possible solutions to help resolve the problems. Every idea is valuable, and you can write them all down.

3. PROPOSE A SOLUTION. After looking at all the options, decide—as a family—a good solution that works for everyone. Put this into practice during the week and check in at the next meeting to discuss if it worked.

4. PLAN A FAMILY ACTIVITY. Take turns sharing your interests and needs as a family to decide on an activity to do as a team.

5. DECIDE ON AN ACTIVITY. Choosing an activity can be assigned to a different person every week, or you can choose one from the jar from Activity 83.

6. REFLECTING. At the meeting, every person can ask themselves:

DID YOU KNOW?

The idea of a family meeting comes from Positive Discipline for Families by Jane Nelsen and Lynn Lott.

What did I do this week to try to use the solutions we proposed last week?

If this didn't solve the problem, what can I do to help find a solution?

7. FAMILY MOMENT. It is nice to end the meeting as it began, with positivity and balance. An activity or game that lasts no more than 10 minutes can be enough to create a feeling of harmony and connection.

If it is your first family meeting, you can do another round of gratitude.

You can use an object to help people take turns talking, for example, a microphone (it doesn't have to be functional; its function is just to give someone a turn to talk).

You can find what you need for family meetings on our website. See note on page 4.

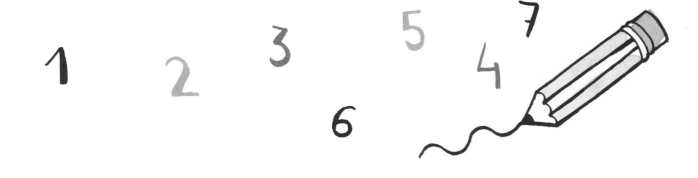

97 Recycling Center

❄ ✿ ☀ 🍁 2+ years
🕐 20 minutes

You don't need to play a complicated game to have fun learning about recycling. Let's set the scene.

Set up bins that correspond to the following categories: food waste, paper, plastic and cans, glass, trash, and recycling center. Collect a variety of items that can be sorted by material and put in the correct container. Each bin can have a drawing attached that shows what kind of waste belongs in that bin.

You can find stickers for your recycling center and a guide for how to recycle your objects on our website. See note on page 4.

98 Reusable Bags for the Pantry

❄ ✿ ☀ 🍁 5+ years
🕐 15–20 minutes

For this activity, you will be using 10 x 11.5 inches (25 x 30 cm) cotton/tote bags and fabric paint. The idea is to work as a family to organize the pantry. What's better than working together as a team! Decorate the bags to help store pasta, dry fruit, or vegetables. You can bring these bags with you to the supermarket to shop in bulk and cut down on using plastic bags.

For example, you can write "Pasta" and then draw macaroni and so on for the other items. Use your imagination!

99 Making Popcorn

❄ ✿ ☀ 🍁 4+ years
🕐 20 minutes

You will need a pot with a lid, popcorn kernels, olive oil, and salt. Heat the oil, add the kernels, and cover, listening for the pop-pop of the kernels. Take the popped kernels out of the pot, and don't worry if some of them didn't pop.

If you prefer, you can substitute butter for the oil, or sugar, honey, or curry powder instead of the salt. There are endless possibilities, depending on what you like! Any flavor is perfect for a family afternoon!

100 Bobbing for Apples

❄ ❁ ☀ 🍁 4+ years

🕐 15 minutes

You will need a bucket of water, and to place some apples in the water. Everyone takes a turn trying to catch an apple using only their mouth. To increase the laughs, set a timer! Remember that the most important thing is to have fun, and no one wins if they complete the activity faster. At the end, you can count how many apples you have caught as a family. If the apples are a little bruised at the end of this, you can make an apple pie or roast them in the oven. Work as a team!

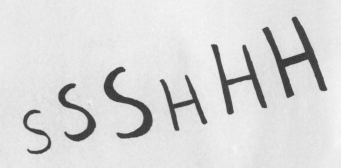

101 The Quiet Game

❄ ❁ ☀ 🍁 3+ years

🕐 15–20 Minutes (depending on willpower)

For this activity, you will use a bell or a lit candle. If you use the bell, explain: "When you hear the bell, close your eyes and pay attention to the sounds you hear."

If you would rather use the candle, you can say: "You are going to try to stay as still as the flame of this candle."

Once the silent time is over, you can talk about the experience. One by one, each person can describe what they heard and how they felt.

102 Catching Oranges with Your Knees

❄ ❁ ☀ 🍁 4+ years

🕐 15 minutes

Put a hoop on the ground and place oranges inside. Take turns kneeling down and trying to pick the oranges up using only your knees. Try to carry the oranges outside of the circle! It is difficult but very fun to try and amusing to watch.

(103) Sensory Socks

❄ ✿ ☀ 🍂 **4+ years**

🕐 10 minutes

Collect as many socks as you want to use, and make sure they don't have any holes. Fill them with lentils, seeds, beans, or anything else that you think of. Sit the family around a big table and fill the socks, tying off the top end to keep the fillings inside. You can use toilet paper rolls as a funnel to help fill the socks. Use the filled socks to play guessing games or to squeeze to relieve stress.

(104) Switching Roles

❄ ✿ ☀ 🍂 **5+ years**

🕐 15 minutes

For this game, you will need clothes from every family member. Take turns choosing articles of clothing and making different outfits spread out on the table, floor, or bed: pants, vests, skirts, shirts, shoes, gloves, hats—whatever you like! No one can choose their own clothes. Adults can even end up with the children's clothes!

(105) Listen to Music Lying Down

❄ ✿ ☀ 🍂 **4+ years**

🕐 10 minutes

Find a mat for each family member. Lie down, close your eyes, and put on some music to listen to. Relax. Afterward, sit up and talk about how you felt or if any piece of music stood out and felt special. Two people can feel completely different about the same song!

(106) Sensory Walkway

❋ ☼ 🍃 **12+ months**
🕐 10 minutes

Create a path outside with different trays, set one after the other, as if they were tiles. Put different textured items in each tray: grass, dry leaves, flour, muesli, pebbles. Start at the beginning and try standing in each tray all the way to the end.

(107) Experiment with Oranges

❄ ❋ ☼ 🍃 **4+ years**
🕐 10 minutes

Will an orange float with or without its peel?

Let's compare! Get a bowl of water and fill it with water. Peel one orange and leave the other whole. Put the oranges in the bowl of water. Which one floats? Before putting the oranges in the bowl, each family member can form their hypothesis and test it. What is it that makes one float and the other sink? This activity can be done with other fruits and vegetables to see whether there are differences. Let's find out!

(108) Painting with Shaving Cream

❄ ❋ ☼ 🍃 **2+ years**
🕐 10 minutes

You will need shaving cream, food coloring, mixing bowls, and a roll of paper. Mix the shaving cream with the different colors and begin painting!

Remember that shaving cream is not edible. It is only for painting!

(109) walk in a Line

❄ ✿ ☀ 🍁 **3+ years**

🕐 10 minutes

Take turns walking in a line. You can make the line with tape, and you can make it more difficult as the activity progresses.

For example, begin by walking in the line empty-handed. Next, carry a small book flat in your hands, and then add a glass of water you need to try not to spill, or an egg that can't roll and fall.

DID YOU KNOW?

An ellipse drawn on the floor is common in a Montessori environment. This is for children to practice walking on. The ellipse isn't a uniform shape, since it has a long side and a short side, which makes it perfect to practice walking carefully without leaving the line.

110 Alphabet Lids

❄ ✿ ☀ 🍁 **4–5+ years**

🕐 15 minutes

Collect all the spare lids you have in the house to make a fun word game. Write one letter of the alphabet on each lid with a permanent marker, and group different lids together to form words like names, animals, objects, etc.

You can also try collecting random lids and seeing what words you can make from them. If you're not sure if a word exists, you can always look it up in the dictionary.

To make this easier, make some extra lids with common letters like vowels.

111 What Feeling is on my Head?

❄ ✿ ☀ 🍁 **14+ months**

🕐 20 minutes

This activity is to help us learn to express ourselves. To do this, find a headband or rubber band and cards that have different feelings written on them. To make it even simpler, you can use emojis like: happy :) sad :(disgust D; fear :S or anger >:[for example. Or a mix of others!

Choose a card and, without looking, strap it to your head with the headband. The objective is to guess what feeling you have on your forehead by asking other family members a series of questions.

You can find feelings cards and drawings on our website. See page note on page 4.

112 Elephant Game

❄ ✿ ☀ 🍁 **4+ years**

🕐 10 minutes

You will need a stocking, an orange, and empty plastic water bottles.

On one side, put the bottles standing on the floor. You can put them in a triangle like bowling pins, in a straight line, or whatever other shape you like. Then put the orange inside the stocking and push it down to the toe. Then, taking turns, pull the other end of the stocking over your head so the toe with the orange in it hangs down. Using your head to swing the orange, see how many water bottles you can knock down. You can do this with or without moving your feet; the important thing is to swing the orange! The laughs are guaranteed!

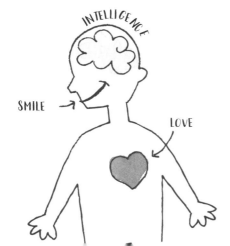

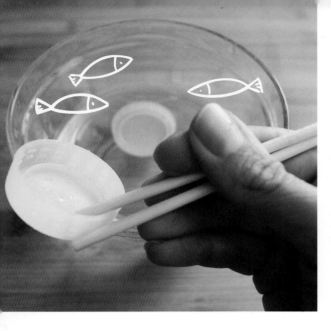

(113) Fishing for Lids

❄ ✿ ☀ 🍁 4+ years
🕐 10 minutes

For this activity, you will need a bowl of water, a variety of different-sized plastic caps and lids that will float, and a pair of chopsticks. Put a time limit on each turn, and take turns trying to pick up the lids with the chopsticks. To increase the difficulty level, limit everyone to only using one hand. When the time is up, count how many lids you have been able to fish out of the bowl.

(114) Covered in Post-Its

❄ ✿ ☀ 🍁 6+ years
🕐 10 minutes

Take turns sticking Post-Its to each other. Every person gets one minute to stick as many as they can. Once the time limit is up, count how many Post-Its you have on your body. You can increase the difficulty by writing positive qualities on each Post-It before sticking it. A different virtue on each Post-It, what a self-esteem boost!

(115) Disco Night

❄ ✿ ☀ 🍁 2+ years
🕐 15 minutes

Everyone knows a good dance party needs colored lights to set the scene for a spectacular night. These lights are easy to make: just cover your lamps and lights with colored cellophane paper. Then put on music and dance under the lights of your DIY disco!

(116) Spoon Transfer

❄ ✿ ☀ 🍁 14+ months
🕐 10 minutes

You will need two bowls, one filled with small balls and one empty. Take turns trying to move the balls from one bowl to the other. If you want to make it a little more complicated, you can hold the spoon with your mouth. The result? A time spent having fun and laughing!

(117) Home Bookstore

❄ ✾ ☀ 🍁 **2+ years**

🕐 20 min

Pretend games make up a large part of childhood, and without a doubt, our small children enjoy playing these games with their reference people, their family. Use your home collection of stories to encourage reading through this family game: a bookstore at home!

It's simple. Gather all your favorite books and assign roles to each family member: booksellers and readers!

You can find materials to make your bookstore on our website. See note on page 4.

MATERIALS

- Books, stories, and magazines
- Tickets for currency (you can use the ones created in Activity 37)
- Display to show the books and stories
- Cash register for the tickets

DID YOU KNOW?

They say that, in Egypt, libraries were called "the treasury of soul remedies," because within them you could cure ignorance.

"Books give roads and days to wise people."

Proverb

(118) Match Socks

❄ ✿ ☀ 🍁 2+ years
🕐 15 minutes

Gather your socks. Spread them out on a surface and look for pairs. Did you find them?

(120) Tea Party

❄ ✿ ☀ 🍁 2+ years
🕐 15–20 minutes

Time to dust off the kettle and the teacups, because it is time for a tea party!

This is not pretend; this is for real! Prepare a special tea for each person, depending on their age.

Set up a special area for your tea party, using items that will set the scene. A tablecloth, some napkins and fun music, and you are ready!

(119) Family Wall

❄ ✿ ☀ 🍁 9+ months
🕐 20 minutes

A family wall is a central point for information about the family, where you can find each person.

Here is where you can address issues that affect the whole family and your home like meals, routines, or daily work, and you can make a visual representation of all these actions.

This wall can serve whatever function you need it to within your family. You can use a blackboard, a whiteboard, or a magnet board to put a weekly menu, for example, reminders, or a shopping list. You can put a yearly calendar to remember important dates, or a mailbox to collect suggestions to bring to your family meeting. You can use it to display artwork made by family members, and let every member contribute their work.

→ DID YOU KNOW?

"Afternoon Tea" is a British custom, where you can not only have some tea but also a light dinner. Their etiquette dictates that sipping or blowing on the tea is considered rude, despite the tea being very hot. Instead, to cool their tea, they stir the cup with a spoon.

121 Ice Painting

❄ ✿ ☀ 🍁 14+ months

🕐 10 minutes

Take a few bowls of water and add different colors of food coloring to them. Pour each color into ice cube trays. Stick popsicle sticks into each mold and freeze.

Once the trays are frozen, use the ice cubes to paint. Remember to freeze them with the popsicle sticks in so you can use those to hold the cubes and not freeze your fingers holding the ice cube!

122 Veterinary Clinic

❄ ✿ ☀ 🍁 2+ years

🕐 15 minutes

Make a veterinary clinic for all your stuffed animals. Let's make some veterinarian hats out of paper! Gather bandages and bandaids, make a stethoscope by attaching two funnels with a tube or an empty container of yogurt, get paper and pen to write prescriptions, bottles for medicine, and get to work on those stuffed animals. Let's help them all!

You can find materials for your veterinary clinic on our website. See note on page 4.

123 Bathing the Baby

❄ ✿ ☀ 🍁 2+ years

🕐 15 minutes

Let your child bring their favorite water-resistant doll to their bath time and bathe it like a baby. They can perform their whole bath time routine with it, and dry it off with a towel and give it a fresh change of clothes just like a real bath.

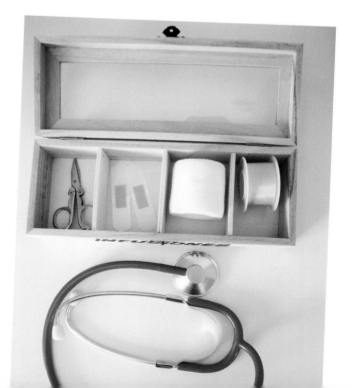

(124) Daily Chores

❄ ✿ ☀ 🍂 **3+ years**

🕐 15 minutes

Everyone in the family needs to be conscious of the importance of working together on household chores like setting the table, doing the dishes, sweeping, mopping, or taking out the trash. One simple way to tackle these chores is to make a chart where you can write the name of each task and draw an illustration for each one. Each family member can choose an activity to do every day. Keep it from being an obligation and let it be flexible!

You can find a chore chart and drawings on our website. See note on page 4.

(125) Frozen Fossils

❄ ✿ ☀ 🍂 **3+ years**

🕐 10 minutes

Take a balloon and put a small object inside: a small toy, a coin, a rock, a flower, etc. Fill the balloon with water and put it in the freezer for a few hours. Once it is fully frozen, take it out and cut the balloon off to find a giant ice ball with the small object inside. To get the object out, run the ball under hot water to melt the ice and find your artifact.

(126) Family Sticker Album

❄ ✿ ☀ 🍂 **4+ years**

🕐 30 minutes

Pick out photos of trips, food, family moments, and people who make up your family. Print them, cut them out, and stick them to a piece of cardboard folded like a small book. Sit together around the table and fill this album with clippings for your family, talking about the events and people in the pictured moments, what happened, what you did, and the most important parts you don't want to forget. Above all, enjoy the activity and the connection!

(127) Self-Portrait

❄ ✽ ☀ 🍁 **4+ years**

🕐 20 minutes

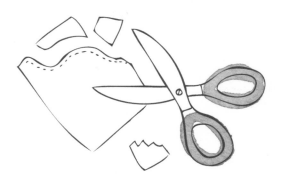

This is a very special family craft. Anyone who wants to make a portrait can cut their silhouette out of cardboard. Let's make a self-portrait!

Collect different objects and materials like buttons for eyes, mouths cut out of cardboard, string for hair, and construction paper for the nose.

Make a family portrait, gluing the pieces onto the cardboard. Do you see the resemblance?

(128) Apple Sandwiches

❄ ✽ ☀ 🍁 **2+ years**

🕐 10 minutes

Cut apples into rings, two for each sandwich you are going to make. Spread peanut butter, almond butter, hazelnut spread, or cheese onto each slice and top with the other apple slice. Snack time!

(129) Tightrope Walker

❄ ✽ ☀ 🍁 **4+ years**

🕐 15 minutes

Make two parallel lines on the floor with tape. One end is the start and the other is the finish. Using a fly swatter, tap the balloon and transport it from one end of the line to the other without stepping off the line. Do this like a relay race, with the next person waiting for you to complete the activity before they go, until every member of the family has had a turn and everyone has become an expert balloon-carrying tightrope walker!

(130) Paper Cup Tower

❄️ 🌸 ☀️ 🍁 3+ years

🕐 20 minutes

Let's make a paper cup tower with the whole family. How tall can you make it before it falls down?

(131) Draw Yourself in the Mirror

❄️ 🌸 ☀️ 🍁 5+ years

🕐 10 minutes

Put a mirror in front of each family member. You will be looking at your reflection. Use temporary markers for glass to draw yourself on the surface of the mirror.

(132) Wish Board

❄️ 🌸 ☀️ 🍁 4–5+ years

🕐 15 minutes

Any free space on the wall can become a wish board. Put up a chalkboard or dry erase board, and keep Post-Its and markers of different colors for each family member to express their wishes. These wishes can be for the family, for the world, or for each individual. Once they've been written, stick them up on the board. This activity can be done at any moment, or on a special date like on New Year's.

You can find a template for your wish board on our website. See note on page 4.

(133) Sumo Cushions

❄️ 🌸 ☀️ 🍁 5+ years

🕐 20 minutes

Each family member needs a large shirt about four sizes bigger than their usual size. Put a cushion inside the shirt and let's sumo wrestle! The objective is to knock the other person onto the couch. I AS-SUMO that you know how challenging this will be!

(134) Linear Calendar

❄ 🌼 ☀ 🍁 **4+ years**

🕐 1 hour

For small children, the passing of time is abstract and difficult to understand. You can assist them with processing these ideas by making a linear calendar, constructing it horizontally at eye level along a wall.

The linear calendar can help us visualize a whole year. You can make this calendar out of sheets of paper, one next to the other. Mark them with the number of the month. This can help us see not only the days of the week or the months, but also the seasons and holidays. You can mark these special events with writing and drawing on little Post-Its.

You can find a linear calendar on our website. See note on page 4.

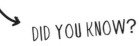

DID YOU KNOW?

The linear calendar is a resource inspired by the Montessori theory of education's concept of the passing of time.

(135) Telephone Game

❄ 🌼 ☀ 🍁 **4+ years**

🕐 10 minutes

Who hasn't played this game? Everyone sits in a circle and the first person whispers a phrase in the ear of the next person. They whisper it to the next person and so on, all around the circle. The last person says the phrase out loud to the group. Is it the same phrase that was said at the beginning?

(136) Human Knot

❄ 🌼 ☀ 🍁 **4+ years**

🕐 20 minutes

One person leaves the room and the rest stand in a circle. Reach out and grab the hand of someone else until everyone is holding hands with a different person and have created a human knot. The person who left comes back in and their job is to guide everyone's movements until the knot is untangled, without anyone letting go of their hands. The more people you are able to include, the better!

Enjoying the City as a Family

1 LEARN ABOUT YOUR ENVIRONMENT

Sometimes we travel very far to learn about other places, but we forget that the place closest to us is perfect for exploring and learning. This is the first place outside of our home that our children will discover.

2 CULTURE

Cities and towns give us access to the cultural parts of society. You can learn about customs, traditions, and ideas. There are so many ways to discover and learn about the cultures that surround us and to participate in what the city has to offer.

3 HISTORY

You can learn about the history of a place, about the civilizations that came before you. The stories of your grandparents.

4 SOCIETY

Learn how to put our social skills into practice, saying "thank you," "please," "hello," and "goodbye."

5 CONVENIENCE

You have access to so many services and activities.

6 ART

Creativity and art is everywhere in the city. Urban art, bit by bit, is becoming more important and available for our enjoyment.

137 City Kit

❄ ❀ ☀ 🍁 2+ years

🕐 20 minutes

The city kit is a great tool to bring with you for the whole family. It can be of great assistance when you leave the house.

What goes in the kit? The first thing you will need is a backpack where you can put everything you need.

Fill the backpack with items that invite you to imagine, create, and have fun: pictures, notebook, magnifying glass, travel games, a plastic ball and a mini puzzle. It is important that everything be small and lightweight since you'll be carrying it a lot!

When should you use the kit? You will need this kit during times where there isn't a lot to do: when you are waiting in a restaurant, at the doctor's office, or in traffic.

MATERIALS

- Pictures
- Notebook
- Magnifying Glass
- Travel Game
- Plastic Ball
- Mini Puzzle

CITY
KIT

138 Observe an Anthill

❀ ☀ 🍁 **14+ months**

🕐 10 minutes

Certainly there is an anthill somewhere near your house. Embrace this opportunity! Observing an anthill can be very entertaining, and afterward, you can find more information about what you've seen. Did you know ants can carry up to fifty times their own weight?

139 Types of Kisses (Eskimo, Butterfly, Cow)

❄ ❀ ☀ 🍁 **14+ months**

🕐 10 minutes

There are so many kinds of kisses: eskimo or gnome (rubbing noses), butterfly (brushing eyelashes), or cow (slobbery with your tongue!). Can you invent your own? Do you have your own family kiss? Let's kiss!

MWAH

140 Feed the Pigeons

❄ ❀ ☀ 🍁 **18+ months**

🕐 10 minutes

Pigeons are everywhere in the city. If you want to see them, all you have to do is take out some stale bread, and in a few seconds, you'll be surrounded by pigeons!

(141) Crosswalks

❄️ 🌼 ☀️ 🍁 18+ months

🕐 10 minutes

How many crosswalks do you walk through every day? More than you could believe! What if you had to jump from white line to white line? Always play this with an adult! If you want to add an extra challenge, try it on one leg!

→ DID YOU KNOW?

Crosswalks existed even in Ancient Rome. Instead of being painted on the ground, they were marked with giant blocks with enough room for vehicles' wheels to pass through.

(142) Observing Snails

❄️ 🌼 ☀️ 🍁 2+ years

🕐 10 minutes

Like ants, snails also live in the city. You can observe them leaving their trail, how they hide, when they come out of hiding, and what times they are easy to find.

Pssst! A good time to find them is after a big rain.

(143) Visit a Museum

❄️ 🌼 ☀️ 🍁 4–5+ years

🕐 30 minutes

Museums are great options for exploring culture in the city. You can visit familiar galleries or traveling exhibitions. Whenever you feel like it, you can visit new spaces. There are all kinds. Let's try to visit them all!

(144) Visit a Library

❄ ✿ ☀ 🍁 3–4+ years

🕐 20 minutes

Going to the library is always a great option for having some quiet fun and spend time surrounded by books. You can find tons of stories and tales to live and feel, to learn about responsibility, and to take home a book and return it. And you will surely find lots of small treasures.

(145) Train Adventure

❄ ✿ ☀ 🍁 3–4+ years

🕐 10 minutes

Sometimes the rhythm of the city can be a bit oppressive. Everyone who lives in the city is used to taking public transportation for fun or for work: What is it like to take a train with just the simple objective to enjoy the trip? Learn how to travel by train, how many stops it will take, what to do when you get to your stop, how to get off the train, and a million other details that are fun to learn as a family.

(146) Go to a Musical

❄ ✿ ☀ 🍁 4–5+ years

🕐 1 hour

One way to disconnect from the hustle and bustle of the city without going very far is to go to the theater. Leave your routine and absorb yourself in a musical and enjoy the spectacle!

(147) Visit a Botanical Garden

❄ ✿ ☀ 🍁 **3+ years**

🕒 25 minutes

Sometimes nature can feel a little far from the city, so a great idea can be to visit a botanical garden and enjoy the variety of plants and flowers that you can find there.

(148) Visit a Farmers' Market

❄ ✿ ☀ 🍁 **14+ months**

🕒 10 minutes

A farmers' market is, without a doubt, one of the best places to practice manners. Saying hello, learning how to ask for things and how to say thank you. You can learn how to take turns and how to wait. This is an enriching experience to put our social habits to the test.

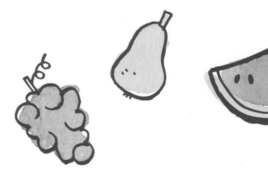

(149) Play in the Sprinklers

✿ ☀ **14+ months**

🕒 10 minutes

If you are in the park and the sprinklers turn on, why stay away? If it is a very hot day, you can enjoy them and feel refreshed. Take advantage of every moment you can find!

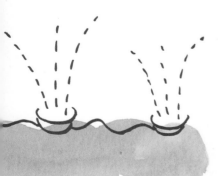

(150) Reusing Napkins

❄ ✳ ☀ 🍁 **4+ years**

🕐 20 minutes

For this activity, you only need a napkin holder, chalk paint, and sheets of paper.

Paint the napkin holder with the chalk paint and cut the paper to the size of napkins, cutting as many as the napkin holder will fit.

Once you have cut the paper, you can make drawings and keep them in the napkin holder, accumulating all these pieces of art.

This is an excellent way to collect and display artwork.

MATERIALS

- Napkin Holder
- Chalk Paint (whatever color you like)
- Sheets of paper
- Scissors
- Drawings

DID YOU KNOW?

They say that Leonardo Da Vinci invented the napkin. In an effort to keep diners from dirtying the table cloth where they ate, he offered a cloth to each person at the table so they could wipe their hands.

151 Enjoying a Meal in a Restaurant

❄ ❀ ☀ 🍂 4+ years

🕐 10 minutes

A meal in a restaurant can be an odyssey or an adventure. Anticipating things is always helpful, especially when the whole family is involved in the planning. Where should we go? What can we bring with us in case we are bored? Who will order for us when the waiter comes to the table?

152 Excursion on a Tourist Bus Around the City

❄ ❀ ☀ 🍂 4–5+ Years

🕐 10 minutes

How long have you lived in your city without enjoying a trip on a tourist bus? Now is the time! It is fun to listen to the guide and learn things about the city you didn't already know.

153 Play "I Spy"

❄ ❀ ☀ 🍂 4+ years

🕐 10 minutes

You don't need to invest a lot in this game. It is an excellent opportunity to come together as a family and enjoy a moment wherever you are! "I spy with my little eye, something beginning with the letter . . ." and enjoy!

154 Chasing Pigeons

❄ ✿ ☀ 🍁 14+ months

🕐 5 minutes

It can be very fun to run up to a flock of pigeons, see how they fly up into the air, and feel the wind from their wings.

DID YOU KNOW?

Pigeons' eyes change color as they get older. When they are just born, their eyes are brown or gray and when they are adults, they turn orange.

155 Puddle Jumping

❄ ✿ ☀ 🍁 12+ months

🕐 5 minutes

Don't hide from the rain or the puddles! Put on some good rain boots and raincoat and enjoy the rainy days!

156 Skating

❄ ✿ ☀ 🍁 4+ years

🕐 10 minutes

On asphalt, ice, or on a track, whatever place you want to skate that you can find. Get your safety gear and a hand to hold and get ready to laugh!

(157) Visit Family

❄ ✿ ☀ 🍁 **12+ months**

🕐 10 minutes

Why not! Without any special reason, just to enjoy their company. You can always bring something for lunch or a snack, or another kind of gift. They will be thrilled!

(158) Visit a Climbing Wall

❄ ✿ ☀ 🍁 **5–6+ years**

🕐 20 minutes

There are no mountains in the city, but you can always find a place to climb. Follow the safety rules and have fun with your family. Nothing can stop you from finding an adventure!

(159) Read the Signs You Find

❄ ✿ ☀ 🍁 **4–5+ years**

🕐 15 minutes

Walk around the city and find a game at every corner, like reading the signs you find. What is the most original? The longest? The strangest?

(160) Visit a Senior Living Residence

❄ ✿ ☀ 🍁 6+ years

🕐 30 minutes

Spend some time at a senior living residence reading the paper with a senior citizen, listening to their stories, and learning a bit about them. Connecting with older people who were also once young children is nourishing for them and for us.

(161) Go Out for Ice Cream

❄ ✿ ☀ 🍁 12+ months

🕐 10 minutes

What a fun day! A day when getting covered in chocolate (or whatever flavor you prefer!) is part of the plan.

(162) Take an Urban Art Tour

❄ ✿ ☀ 🍁 5–6+ years

🕐 10 minutes

Lots of art in the city is painted on walls, spectacular murals everywhere. But have you stopped to look at them? This is a great occasion to pay more attention and look at some special art.

(163) Juggling

❄ ✳ ☀ 🍁 **4+ years**

🕐 25 minutes

Fill some big socks or colorful stockings with rice (you can use a cup or a funnel to help), pressing it so it is compact, and make a knot so it doesn't spill. Now you're ready! You have your juggling balls. Time to practice!

MATERIALS

- Two long socks or stockings (used)
- Rice
- Funnel or cup

DID YOU KNOW?

It seems that the first signs of jugglers date back to Ancient Egypt when they found an inscription in the stone of a pharaoh's tomb showing this kind of game. The name of the pharaoh was Beni Hassan.

(164) Rock, Paper, Scissors

❄ ✿ ☀ 🍁 3–4+ Years

🕐 10 minutes

This is a well-known game and has been passed down from generation to generation.

To play this game, you need two people. Each person hides their hand behind their back, and at the same time, they say, "Rock, paper, scissors" and take out their hand showing one of these elements: scissors (the hand pointing fingers like a pair of scissors), paper (the hand is held flat like a sheet of paper), or rock (the hand is closed in a fist like a rock). The scissors cut paper, the rock is heavy and breaks the scissors, and the paper covers the rock. Now that we know this, we can play nonstop!

(165) Attend a Play

❄ ✿ ☀ 🍁 4–5+ years

🕐 1 hour

Going to a play helps us disconnect from our routines, our daily life, the hustle and bustle of the city. In this moment, in this place, you can enjoy creativity, novelty, let your feelings come to the surface, and share this with the people we love the most, our family.

(166) Visit a Flea Market

❄ ✿ ☀ 🍁 5+ years

🕐 30 minutes

Enjoy antiques, relics, and historical objects. Walk through stalls filled with treasures in a nostalgic open-aired market that you can visit with your family.

(167) Ride a Carousel

❄ ❀ ☀ 🍁 **12+ months**

🕐 10 minutes

It is never too late! Take the opportunity to remember your childhood while creating new memories for your children.

(168) Have a Picnic in a Park

❄ ❀ ☀ 🍁 **12+ months**

🕐 10 minutes

All you need for this activity is to prepare a good picnic in a basket and head to the park to enjoy it!

(169) Hidden Treasures

❄ ❀ ☀ 🍁 **2+ years**

🕐 25 minutes

Find some rocks and paint them with the whole family. Find places around the city to leave them for other lucky people to find!

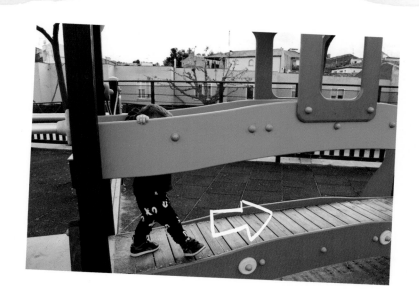

(170) Follow the Chain

❄ ✿ ☼ 🍁   6+ years

🕐 15 minutes

Let's do a social experiment with the family: the idea is to, for example, leave a book on a bench with a sign that says: "Pick up and leave somewhere else." Leave it for the morning and return to see what has happened. With no kind of expectation, only curiosity, the experience and not knowing what will happen will determine the course of this experiment.

(171) Donate Toys/Clothes/ Food

❄ ✿ ☼ 🍁   4+ years

🕐 15 minutes

Any time is a good time to be caring and altruistic. All you need to do is to be conscious of the realities that surround us and to help the people who need it. You don't always have to go far to find someone who needs help: your friend, neighbor, or someone close can benefit from sharing resources.

(172) Go to a Concert

❄ ✿ ☼ 🍁   4+ years

🕐 1 hour

Let the music surround you! Some smiles, dancing, and dinner under the lights!

(173) Walk in a Train

❄ ✿ ☀ 🍁 2+ years

🕐 10 minutes

At times, walking on the street can feel long, and in these moments, you can try things to make it a little more fun like forming a human train: one person behind the other walking the way you need to go. It is important not to be embarrassed! It is more fun when you gesture and make the sounds of a train.

(174) Share and Propose

❄ ✿ ☀ 🍁 5+ years

🕐 10 minutes

Think of a café in your neighborhood or a place where you can go to have a snack. Think about these questions: Is this place set up for children? Are there small seats or adaptable tables? Are there toys and books? Maybe you can bring some toys from your house to give to the café to help it be more comfortable.

(175) Go Shopping at the Supermarket

❄ ✿ ☀ 🍁 2+ years

🕐 20 minutes

Before going shopping, make a list of everything you need. If your children are too young to read or write, try making some drawings for them on a piece of paper. If they can read or write, make a list that is clear and easy to read. You can even bring a calculator in addition to the list so they can calculate the costs and figure out if you can afford an impulse purchase on the given budget.

You can find a template for your list on our website. See note on page 4.

DID YOU KNOW?

In other times, the currency of exchange was more of a barter system: "I can give you what you need, and you can give me what I need." But this became harder to use with the growth of commercial activity and people didn't always need what others were offering. And oftentimes, the items or services being exchanged didn't always have the same value, which makes it difficult to work well. This is how money came into being.

(176) Cleaning the City

❄ ❀ ☀ 🍁 **2+ years**

🕐 20 minutes

How many times have you walked around your neighborhood and found paper thrown all over the ground? And if this is the case, do you pick it up? Here is an idea! Get some big tongs and go out into the street to collect trash from the ground. Always dispose of your trash correctly. You can turn this into a fun activity and feel happy knowing you are doing something nice for your neighborhood and for your neighbors. The next time you see someone throwing trash on the ground, invite them to throw it away properly.

MATERIALS

- Long tongs
- Short tongs
- Trash can or bag
- Gloves

DID YOU KNOW?

The cleanest cities in the world are in Canada, specifically Calgary. This is achieved by having strict fines. Is this the only way to solve the problem of trash in our streets?

"What will happen to us if we destroy the environment around us? Let caring be our mantra!"

Zazu Navarro

(177) Red Light, Green Light

❄ ❀ ☀ 🍁 4+ years

🕐 20 minutes

Waiting can feel like an eternity sometimes, but you can always use this time to play a little game like "Red Light, Green Light." This game has many different names, but the idea is always the same. This game is most fun with four or more people. One person faces the wall and starts by saying "green light!" at which point the other players walk (no running!) taking steps toward the wall. The person facing the wall then calls out "red light!" signaling the other players to freeze. The person facing the wall turns around quickly, and if they see anyone still moving, that person has to go back to the starting line. The goal of the game is to touch the wall without being caught running a red light!

(178) Attend a Sports Game

❄ ❀ ☀ 🍁 5+ years

🕐 1 hour

Are there any sports teams playing in your city or town? Let's go cheer them on while they play!

(179) Folding Napkins

❄ ❀ ☀ 🍁 2+ years

🕐 5 minutes

When you're at a bar or a restaurant, there are a lot of opportunities to wait. Practice folding the napkins into different shapes: a bird, a boat, a pacifier, whatever shape you think of.

(180) Draw with Chalk in the Park

❄ ❀ ☀ 🍁 18+ months

🕐 10 minutes

Drawing with chalk is a fun way to make temporary art anywhere. Bring some chalk with you to the park and have fun drawing faces, tracing shadows, writing words, and whatever messages you want to share with people who walk by and see it. What kind of message do you want to reflect? Use your imagination!

DID YOU KNOW?

Do you know why chalk screeches sometimes when you are drawing with it? Depending on the angle you are holding the chalk, it can make little hops against the surface instead of moving smoothly. This sound gives us goosebumps!

(181) Give Flowers to Passersby

❄ ❀ ☀ 🍁 2+ years

🕐 10 minutes

You can find wildflowers all over the city that aren't in someone's garden or on private property. Pick some of these flowers and hand them out to people you see. You don't have to know someone to give them a flower and make them smile. This can really change someone's day and doesn't cost a thing!

(182) Visit an Animal Refuge

❄ ❀ ☀ 🍁 6+ years

🕐 20 minutes

Animal refuges are places where people take care of animals who need help. If you can find one near your city, it's a great place to learn about how these places work and how your family can help. There are plenty of ways to help besides donating money, like investing some time to help clean, take care of, or cuddle the animals. This is nourishing for people, too!

(183) Jumping Rope

❋ ☀ **5+ years**

🕐 30 minutes

Get ready to jump rope! You will need two people to hold the ropes on each side and to turn them. Each person who participates will go in and out, taking turns, while singing songs.

There are so many varieties of songs and games for jumping rope to explore and practice!

Some jump rope songs and rhymes to try include:

DID YOU KNOW?

It is believed that Egyptians created the jump rope using strings and reeds.

- Cinderella
- Miss Mary Mack
- Fuzzy Wuzzy
- Teddy Bear, Teddy Bear
- K-I-S-S-I-N-G
- Miss Lucy

(184) Visit a Ball Pit

❄ ✿ ☼ 🍁 2+ years

🕐 10 minutes

This is the only pool you can swim in and leave without getting wet. Why don't you try it someday?

(185) Eat at a Food Truck

❄ ✿ ☼ 🍁 3+ years

🕐 15 minutes

This is a fun way to share and enjoy a different kind of meal with your family. Breakfast, lunch, a snack, or a dinner. Whatever you want!

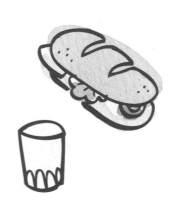

(186) Visit an Amusement Park

❄ ✿ ☼ 🍁 4+ years

🕐 2 hours

Find an amusement park near your city. This is a fun way to enjoy a variety of experiences and emotions!

(187) Visit a Medieval Village

❄️ ☀️ 🌸 🍁   12+ months

🕐 1 hour

Medieval villages can transport us to another time and place: the clothes, decorations, street performances. This is a great way to experience history in person!

(188) Make Water Balloons in the Fountain

☀️   4+ years

🕐 25 minutes

This is going to be super entertaining, but be prepared to get wet! Once you have a pile of water balloons, there is an endless number of activities you can do with them: sit on them until they burst, pass them from person to person hoping they don't fall, juggle them. What else can you think of to do?

(189) See a Storyteller Show

❄️ 🌸 ☀️ 🍁   2+ years

🕐 20 minutes

Stories can transport us to other places without having to travel. Love of reading is something to cultivate and grow, and going to see a storyteller or stopping in for Story Time at your local library is a good way to foster this love of books and reading.

(190) Observing a Puddle

❄ ✿ ☀ 🍁 **4+ years**

🕐 10 minutes

For this activity, you will need to wait until it has rained because you are going to see how long it takes a puddle to dry. First, you will need to find a puddle. Use chalk to trace the shape of the puddle, and then continue to observe it as you pass by throughout the day to see how it is drying.

DID YOU KNOW?

Drops of water are not teardrop-shaped. When they are small, they are globe-shaped, and when they are bigger, they are shaped like a bean. This is due to gravity and the air pressure when they fall.

MATERIALS

- Chalk
- Puddle
- Watch (to time how long it takes to dry)

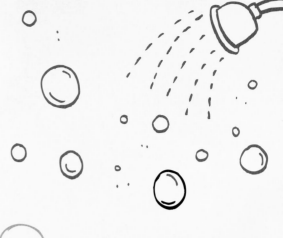

(191) Leave Messages at Cultural Destinations

❄ ✿ ☀ 🍁   6+ years

🕐 15 minutes

Are you going to visit a monument, some ruins, an exposition, a play? A fun thing to do is to have everyone in the family write down a fact about the place and put this paper in an envelope labeled "Please Read Me" and leave it somewhere for someone else to find it. They will have a nice surprise!

(192) Enjoy a Day at the Spa

❄ ✿ ☀ 🍁   10+ years

🕐 1 hour

In the section about activities to do at home, we talked about how to set up a spa at home (Activity 13). Now it is time to visit an actual spa, where you can get a massage or sit in a sauna, and where you can experience all these activities that help you completely relax.

FOR WHOEVER FINDS THIS:

PLEASE READ ME

(193) Go to the Public Pool

✿ ☀ 🍁   12+ months

🕐 15–25 minutes

Visiting the public pool with the whole family can be a lot of fun. If the pool is heated, you can go any day of the year.

(194) Clean the Car

❄ 🌸 ☀ 🍁 3+ years

🕐 5 minutes

Cleaning the car doesn't have to be boring! Turn it into an activity the whole family can enjoy. Whether you're going to the car wash or pulling out your hose, this can become a moment for the whole family to enjoy.

(195) Go to the Skate Park

❄ 🌸 ☀ 🍁 4+ years

🕐 15 minutes

Find the skate park in your city! This activity can be just as fun for people who know how to skateboard as it is for people who don't. You can always learn something new, and find questions to ask, talking to people who have more experience and practice. Spend the day on wheels!

DID YOU KNOW?

The first skate park was built in Florida in 1976.

(196) Have a Snack

❄ 🌸 ☀ 🍁 2+ years

🕐 15–20 minutes

Some activities can happen spontaneously, and this can be one of those. It is always a good time to have a little snack after a walk or just as a way to rest a little at any point in the day.

(197) Road Safety

❄ ✳ ☀ 🍁 **4+ years**

🕐 1 hour

Visiting a road safety park is a great idea to help us safely practice how to cross the street and to learn safety rules. You can also attend specialized talks where the speaker teaches us how to move safely through the city. Learning these rules with the whole family can be fun. Bring your own bike or scooter to add to the fun!

DID YOU KNOW?

The first traffic light was installed in 1868 in the United Kingdom and imitated railroad signs, using sounds to show cars when to stop and go. At night, it was lit with gas lights.

"Better late than never."

Popular saying

(198) Write and Send a Letter

❄ ✿ ☼ 🍁 **5–6+ years**

🕐 25 minutes

Why have we lost this beautiful tradition? Why do we send emails when we can send a real physical letter and save it forever? Take out your pencils and get your hands ready!

(199) Crab Walk Game

❄ ✿ ☼ 🍁 **5–6+ years**

🕐 20 minutes

For this game, you will need to get into a crab walk position: with pincer hands and arched feet, and now you're ready to go! One person starts out as the crab, chasing the other players. If someone is touched by the crab, they become a crab, too. The point is to catch everyone and to turn everyone into crabs. The more players, the more crabs!

(200) Hopscotch

❄ ✿ ☼ 🍁 **4+ years**

🕐 However much time you need

Chalk, please! Draw the standard 8-block hopscotch on the ground. Taking turns, each person throws a rock and sees where it lands. Hopping on one leg, the player hops in each hopscotch square from beginning to end, avoiding the square where the rock landed. In the part of the hopscotch drawing where two blocks are next to each other, the player can use both feet to jump in these blocks at the same time.

The idea is to get all the way to the end and back, collecting your stone as you return to the start.

201 Take an Airplane

❄ ✿ ☀ 🍁 1+ month

🕐 Depends on the length of the flight

Taking an airplane is a whole experience, as much for the preparations as it is for the trip itself. Being responsible for your suitcase, following the signs at the airport, waiting, and once you are in your seat, reading or looking out the window: Where are the clouds? Where is our house? What can we see from this altitude? Why is the horizon line curved and not straight?

202 Visit the "Forest" in the Bushes at the Park

❄ ✿ ☀ 🍁 3+ years

🕐 15 minutes

Sometimes all you need is a little bit of nature and a lot of imagination to create a fun adventure. Go to a park nearby and walk among the trees. What if you were exploring an exotic jungle? What animals would you see on your expedition?

203 Identify the Trees in Your City

❄ ✿ ☀ 🍁 5–6+ years

🕐 30 minutes

There are lots of trees in the city, but do you know which kinds of trees they are? Can you find out their names or what kind of fruit they might grow? It is a great idea to know what kinds of trees surround us. Go around your neighborhood collecting leaves and flowers, and take notes with drawings and words of what kinds of branches and trunks they have. You can keep what you've found between the pages of a book, and when you see another that is the same, this can help you figure out how to identify them.

(204) Handkerchief Game

❄ ✾ ☼ 🍁 4+ years

🕐 20 minutes

This is a popular game that is fun to play in any park or plaza.

For this game, you will need a handkerchief and at least three people, but it will be much more fun with a group of at least five.

The players will form two groups and stand facing each other in two lines, with plenty of space between the facing lines. There must be the same number of people in each line. Everyone is assigned a number so that one player from each team has the same number as a corresponding player on the other team. One person is not included in the separate teams and stands in the middle of the facing lines holding a handkerchief. This player yells out a number, and the people from opposite teams that share that number run as fast as they can to grab the handkerchief first. They must then return to their line without being tagged by the other player.

DID YOU KNOW?

Historically, white handkerchiefs have been used to signal a truce to one's enemy.

(205) Play Tag

❄ ✿ ☀ 🍂 2+ years

🕐 10 minutes

Tag is a simple and fun game to play while you're waiting somewhere. This is a universal game known by many different names around the world. When someone says, "You're it!" the whole world takes off running!

(206) Collecting Leaves

❄ ✿ ☀ 🍂 2+ years

🕐 15 minutes

When leaves are falling from the trees in autumn, collect them and bring them home. You can make a collage with your family, add them to the corner of your home dedicated to the season, or incorporate them into whatever activity you can think to use them for.

(207) Searching for Treasure in the Park

❄ ✿ ☀ 🍂 6+ years

🕐 1 hour

One family member is in charge of hiding the treasure. You can make a map of the park, inventing a story about the origin of the treasure and clues to help find it. The treasure can be an interesting rock that you can decorate to help find. Show this on the map! When the treasure is well hidden, set out as a team to solve the clues and find it.

(208) Hand Clapping Games

❄ ✿ ☀ 🍁 **2+ years**

🕐 10 minutes

Any time, any place, any moment. Hand clapping games are so simple! You can invent a song and clap your hands to the rhythm of the music, changing the force or the speed... high five!

(209) Guess the Feeling

❄ ✿ ☀ 🍁 **2–3+ years**

🕐 15 minutes

Taking turns, one person makes an expression or gestures to demonstrate a feeling. Whoever guesses the feeling takes their turn and has the opportunity to demonstrate a feeling for everyone else to guess. This is a fun way to practice how we express ourselves, and how to pay attention to other peoples' feelings.

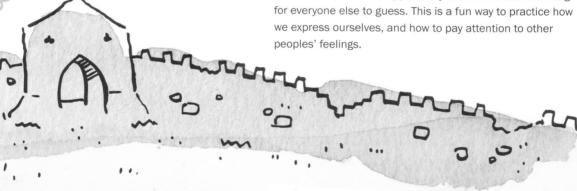

(210) Visit Ruins

❄ ✿ ☀ 🍁 **4+ years**

🕐 30 minutes

There are lots of places to find historic ruins: finding them can be an adventure! Who built this? How? Why? How was it used? Learning is always so enriching!

(211) Facial Expressions in Magazines

❄ ❀ ☀ 🍁 2+ years

🕐 10 minutes

You can usually find magazines in places where people wait, like at the doctor, the dentist, or in a café. Looking through these magazines and newspapers can be a great resource to find fun activities. For example, you can try to identify what all the people in the photographs are feeling, just from looking at their faces or posture. Don't read the text to give it away!

DID YOU KNOW?

The first magazine in the world was a book of articles and was published in Germany between 1663 and 1668.

MATERIALS

- Magazines
- Newspapers

212) Ride a Scooter

❄ ✿ ☀ 🍁 **2+ years**

🕐 10 minutes

Taking a walk is more common, but why not try to switch it up and ride a scooter? This can make the same walks you take every day feel like a totally different activity.

213) See a Music Group

❄ ✿ ☀ 🍁 **12+ months**

🕐 20–25 minutes

Music is life, happiness, and passion. Music is a necessity! Everyone loves to listen to music. Find a music group in your city that you can go see or take a class. See a street performance with your family. And don't forget to dance!

214) Go to a Street Fair

❄ ✿ ☀ 🍁 **12+ months**

🕐 1 hour

There are always festivals in cities and towns that you can enjoy: theater in the street, jugglers, magic, music. If you look, you can find artists showing their art or people performing magic on any corner of the city.

(215) Help at a Soup Kitchen

❄ ✿ ☀ 🍁 6+ years

🕐 1 hour

Look for a soup kitchen near your house where you can lend a hand, get to know people, smile, listen, and share. It is a good opportunity to reflect on what is important.

(216) Word Chain

❄ ✿ ☀ 🍁 6+ years

🕐 15–20 minutes

Taking turns, each person says a word. But here's the thing! Each word has to be related to the last in some way or another, and you can't repeat words. This way you end up creating a chain of related words. At the end, compare the last word to the first and see how different they are!

(217) Play Petanque

❄ ✿ ☀ 🍁 4+ years

🕐 However long you like

Did you know that petanque dates back to Roman Era? And that the word means "feet planted (firmly on the ground)"? It can be very fun to watch how it is played. Pentanque is similar to bocce ball, which you may be more familiar with. Observation is a great way to learn the techniques and mechanics of the game. Once you've learned, you can practice and improve.

(218) The Blind Hen

❄ ✿ ☀ 🍁 **5–6+ years**

🕐 25 minutes

This game is ideal to play in the park or an open space somewhere in the city. The person who is the hen is blindfolded and turned around several times until they are disoriented. Try playing with this dialogue:

PLAYER: Blind Hen, what are you looking for?
BLIND HEN: A needle and a thimble.
PLAYER: Turn around three times and you'll find them!
EVERYONE: One, two three, and back again!

While they say this last phrase, the player who is the hen turns around three times and then back again. Then they need to try to chase the other players, and once they've caught someone, they guess who it is. If they are correct, they change roles.

DID YOU KNOW?

A chicken's beak has lots of nerve endings and is very sensitive. Chickens use their beaks to explore their environment. Is this how the "Blind Hen" game got its name?

(219) wheelbarrow

❄ ✿ ☀ 🍁 **6–7+ years**

🕐 20 minutes

This game is played in pairs. The person who is the wheelbarrow puts their hands on the ground, while their partner picks them up by their feet. Now you can race like this in pairs to reach the finish line.

(220) Visit a Riverbank

❄ ✿ ☀ 🍁 **14+ months**

🕐 20–25 minutes

Take a walk by the river if you can find one close to where you live, and observe how it is, what shape it is, what animals and plants live nearby, and simply enjoy your walk.

(221) Visit a Famous Monument

❄ ✿ ☀ 🍁 **5+ years**

🕐 10 minutes

There is surely a historical monument somewhere close to where you live. It doesn't have to be ancient ruins to be important. There are endless reasons a place could be interesting! Let's discover them!

222 Enjoy a Bike Ride

❄ ✿ ☀ 🍁 14+ months

🕐 1 hour

If you have a bicycle, you can plan a route through the city for the whole family. If you don't, you can always rent one for a few hours. A simple route, with or without destination, and enjoy this journey on wheels!

223 Look at the City from the Tallest Building

❄ ✿ ☀ 🍁 5+ years

🕐 20 minutes

You have seen so much of your city, but have you ever seen it from above? Let's go to the highest point you can find with your family and see your city from above!

224 Create at a Craft Workshop

❄ ✿ ☀ 🍁 2+ years

🕐 1 hour

See if there is a craft workshop in your city, and see if they offer times when you can enjoy the experience with your family!

(225) Draw Shadows

❄ ✾ ☀ 🍁 **2+ years**

🕐 10 minutes

All you need is a sunny day, some chalk, and some company. When you see a shadow appear, STOP! And draw it with your chalk.

MATERIALS

- Sidewalk
- Giant chalk (of all colors)
- Sun
- People and different objects

DID YOU KNOW?

Put a sheet of paper out in the sun. Hold your hand close to the paper. Do you see the shadow? It is clear and defined. Now bring your hand farther away, and watch the shadow fade. Did you know these two kinds of shadows have different names? The more defined shadow is called umbra and the faded shadow is called penumbra.

(226) Stay on the Line

❄ ✽ ☀ 🍁 **3–4+ years**

🕐 10 minutes

You can always find a line or a border on the street or at the park. Practice walking on this line and keeping your balance. Can you walk the whole length without stepping off the line?

(227) Origami

❄ ✽ ☀ 🍁 **5+ years**

🕐 15 minutes

You can always fit a few sheets of paper into your city kit. These will always save you from boredom! Can you make a paper airplane? What adjustments can you make to make it go faster? Can you make a boat that floats on the water? What about birds or frogs? What else can you make?

(228) Go to a Yoga Class

❄ ✽ ☀ 🍁 **2+ years**

🕐 10 minutes

It is important to do things every day to take care of your body and mind, but it is hard to find the time. Why not try something together as a family? It can be very enriching! Look in your city for places where you can practice yoga as a family. Sometimes these are public events in parks or at the beach.

229 Sidewalk Maze

❄ ✿ ☼ 🍁 4+ years

🕐 15 minutes

Draw a maze with chalk on the ground, using different curves and bends to connect the points. On one end, put a rock, and on the other, get ready with your feet. Your mission is to get to the rock by following the line.

230 Phrases with Vowels

❄ ✿ ☼ 🍁 5–6+ years

🕐 15 minutes

Try to create a phrase to repeat that uses a different vowel each time. For example, if the phrase is "The dog runs after the cat," the next person will repeat the phrase replacing all the vowels with "ah." So it would become "Thah dahg rahns ahfter thah chat." Each person can take turns saying the phrase with a different vowel. Once you return to the first vowel, you can change the phrase. Doesn't it make you laugh every time?

231 Pack a Suitcase

❄ ✿ ☼ 🍁 2+ years

🕐 15 minutes

At home, at a hotel, going camping, at a hostel, what do you need to go on a trip? Can you fit it all in your suitcase? For small children, you can make a list using photos of the things you will need.

(232) Cat and Mouse

❄ ❋ ☼ ⚘ **5–6+ years**

🕐 20–25 minutes

This is another simple game that is a lot of fun. You will need at least four people. Choose who is the "mouse" and who is the "cat," and the rest of the players join hands in a circle.

The mouse is inside the circle, and the cat needs to chase them. The players holding hands can keep the cat out of the circle to protect the mouse while singing, "The cat is going to catch you, if not tonight then tomorrow!"

When the cat catches the mouse, they change roles, or you can choose a new cat and mouse.

You'll need more than four people to play this game, since one person will need to be the cat and another a mouse.

DID YOU KNOW?

In ancient Egypt, cats were considered sacred animals. If an Egyptian family's cat died, the whole family would pull out their eyebrows as a sign of mourning.

(233) Take a Ferry

❄ ✿ ☀ 🍁 14+ months

🕐 20 minutes

There may not be a ferry in your city, but if you have the opportunity to take one, it is worth it to experience riding a ferry as a family.

(234) Visit a Traditional Oven

❄ ✿ ☀ 🍁 4+ years

🕐 10 minutes

Though they are few and far between these days, traditional ovens, sometimes referred to as Moorish ovens, still exist in some places. Here you can find history, reminders of past generations, traditional and unique delicacies, and of course, a delicious smell. Bring your appetite!

(235) Jump on a Trampoline

❄ ✿ ☀ 🍁 4+ years

🕐 5 minutes

This is a great form of therapy! It is so fun to jump on a trampoline with your family. Laughter is guaranteed!

(236) Ride on a Cablecar

❄ ✿ ☼ 🍁 **2+ months**

🕐 10 minutes

There is not a cablecar in every city, but if you are lucky enough to visit a place that does or live somewhere nearby, try it out! The views will not disappoint.

(237) The Mirror (Copy Me!)

❄ ✿ ☼ 🍁 **3+ years**

🕐 10 minutes

You can play this game anywhere. One person gestures and the other imitates their gestures silently, acting like a reflection. Try making silly faces and other funny gestures!

BENEFITS OF

Enjoying Nature as a Family

1 UNPLUG

Routines and rushing can keep us from feeling calm and peaceful; contact with nature can be restorative and help us reconnect with these feelings.

2 ATTENTION

Nature can cultivate our attention, freeing the mind and helping us concentrate.

3 MOOD

Our brain can rest while we are away from our daily routines. This can really help improve our mood. Nature is good for your well-being.

4 CREATIVITY

Encouraging creative conflict resolution sets the imagination in motion.

5 FAMILY BONDING

Create positive family moments, and grow your family's bond and connection.

6 MOVEMENT

All of these activities help us get away from our screens and up out of our seats.

(238) Nature Kit

❄ ✿ ☀ 🍁 **18+ months**

🕐 15–20 minutes

A lot goes into planning and organizing activities, including imagining what you will do and preparing everything you will need. One example of this is constructing a nature kit. Take a backpack and fill it with all the tools you will need when out in nature.

A single excursion may not use everything you bring, but it's good to be prepared.

MATERIALS

- Magnifying glass
- Binoculars
- Flashlight
- Ruler or measuring tape
- Jar for observing insects
- Compass
- Notebook
- Pencil
- Book about insects or animals

DID YOU KNOW?

The Amazon is the place with the most biodiversity on the whole planet. Every year, scientists discover new species that live there.

(239) Find Almonds in Bloom

❄️ 🌼 **2+ years**

🕐 25 minutes

You can find almonds in bloom in the winter and spring, between mid-February and March.

Taking a walk among the almond trees, if you live in California, can be not only beautiful but also incredibly educational for everyone in the family. You can observe the life cycle of almond trees, the flower, the fruit and the seed. You can touch them, learn about them, and experience them. This is true of all trees, not just almond trees, no matter where you live!

(240) Pick Flowers

🌼 **18+ months**

🕐 15 minutes

Flowers brighten the landscape, filling it with color. Taking a walk with your family to pick flowers to bring home is a great way to enjoy being outside while learning. What is the name of this flower? What does it smell like? What kind of texture and color does it have? Afterward, you can put them between the pages of a book to press and dry them. There are so many things to do!

(241) Sand Tray

❄️ 🌼 ☀️ 🍁 **3+ years**

🕐 5 minutes

Let your imagination run wild with a tray full of sand where you can draw and set up scenes. In a tray with different compartments, you can put different elements from nature like flowers, pinecones, rocks, sticks, and leaves. Once you have everything all together, go ahead and make art!

(242) Measure the Width of a Tree

❄ ✿ ☀ 🍁 **4+ years**

🕐 3 minutes

In your nature kit (Activity 238), you probably packed a ruler or a measuring tape. They don't take up a lot of space, but they give us a lot of information about the things we find. For example, the width of a tree. What is the perimeter of this tree? How many years old is it? Could it be a hundred years old? And this one? What about this one? Some are so big you have to be creative with how you measure. Sometimes one person's arms don't even fit around the trunk!

(244) Plant a Fruit Tree

❄ ✿ ☀ 🍁 **3+ years**

🕐 20 minutes

Cultivating and watching the fruits of what we plant takes time; seeds don't grow right away and need care and patience. The only way to grow a seed is to take care of it: plant it, water it, solve problems as they occur. The whole family can come together to resolve these issues in the process.

(243) Counting the Rings in a Tree Trunk

❄ ✿ ☀ 🍁 **5–6+ years**

🕐 1 hour

Grooves, lines, stains, and wrinkles are all signs of life that help tell us the age of a tree. These occur throughout a tree's life cycle. It starts as a seed, grows, matures, and at some point, dies. You can read about the life of a tree on a fallen branch or stump, about its past, how long it lived, when it was born, how it fell down. The first year of its life is found at the center of the trunk. In the more humid seasons, the rings are clearer and thicker, while in the drier seasons, the bark grows harder and dry to protect the tree. This is how we can see these dark rings that show each year in the life of a tree.

(245) Run Along the Beach

❄️ 🌼 ☀️ 🍁 2+ years

🕐 10 minutes

The waves of the sea, the breeze, the smell of the salt water, the infinite horizon . . . a beautiful setting to share with the people you love. A trip like this is the definition of freedom. If you have the opportunity, run on the beach. Live in the moment! This is a simple activity and a gratifying way to pass time with your family.

(246) Pick Chestnuts

🍁 2–3+ years

🕐 30 minutes

The woods in autumn are full of wonderful moments. You can prepare a kit to bring with you on a morning or afternoon walk. Gloves, a small basket, long tongs. Afterward, make a family recipe with all the chestnuts you've picked. They are delicious roasted in the oven or on the grill!

(247) Bark Rubbing

❄️ 🌼 ☀️ 🍁 4+ years

🕐 5 minutes

Nature is full of different kinds of textures, and they can sometimes be captured on a piece of paper. Tree trunks have unique shapes and textures. If you put a piece of paper against a trunk and color it with a crayon, you can see the texture of the tree trunk on your paper.

(248) Catch a Bug to Observe

❄ ✿ ☀ 🍁 **12+ months**

🕐 5 minutes

A wide variety of insects live in nature. You can observe them, watch their movements, see where they go and what they do. If you want to investigate them up close, you can catch them carefully in your hands or in a jar and examine them before returning them to their place.

(249) Dreamcatchers

❄ ✿ ☀ 🍁 **2+ years**

🕐 20 minutes

Dreamcatchers are traditional in some Indigenous tribes. They are usually decorated with feathers and beads, and they are hung in homes. In popular culture, they are said to filter dreams and allow only the good ones to get through.

Let's make our own. You will need a round slice of wood, string, an eye hook, and natural decorations. The wood will be the support. At the top, put your eye hook. Next, at the ends of each thread, put a different decoration (feathers, leaves, pinecones, sticks, etc.). Finally, hook them to the hook you will use for hanging. If you want the strings to be separate from each other, you can use tape or staples.

(250) Observe Seashells

❄ ✿ ☀ 🍁 **18+ months**

🕐 25 minutes

One of the most relaxing activities you can do is take a walk by the ocean. On these walks, you can admire the landscape or listen to the sounds of the waves. You can also look for shells and examine them, look at what shape they have, hold them to your ear and ask how they got there.

DID YOU KNOW?

If you are tempted to take a seashell from the beach, remember that other animals need them to survive. Collecting shells from the beach has consequences in that environment, and it can reduce the marine population.

(251) Get Muddy

☀ **12+ months**

🕐 20 minutes

Getting muddy is messy, but it is so much fun to do every once in a while. Why not make a mud puddle on purpose? Wallow in the mud, pile globs on your head, on your arms, crawl, or lie on your back. Laughs are guaranteed!

(252) Plant a Tree

❄ ❀ ☀ 🍁 **2+ years**

🕐 10 minutes

Trees are a magical connection to nature and to our roots. They are life, they give life: without them, we would not exist. Plant a seed or a seedling, water it, take care of it, and watch it grow. These are all wonderful ways to learn about the passing of time.

(253) Roll on the Grass

❀ **2+ years**

🕐 10 minutes

All grownups were once children, and this is why it's always important to play. Rolling in the grass without worrying about getting dirty, lying there with the sun on your face. People who can stay surrounded by childhood have a wonderful treasure, so try to play every day. Don't miss an opportunity! Roll around and enjoy!

254) Make a Snow Cake

❄️ 2+ years

🕐 5 minutes

Obviously, the best cakes are chocolate cakes, but making cake out of snow is much more fun. You can even make it huge, as big as yourself, and decorate it with things you find in nature: sticks, rocks, leaves . . . whatever you can find!

255) Make a Tree Fort

❄️ 🌼 ☀️ 🍁 4+ years

🕐 30 minutes

A secret space, a place to hide, a sanctuary. Make a special place to be! This kind of shelter and experience is important for children, allowing them to create these kinds of spaces to dream. All you need is your imagination and a few other things you can find in nature: sticks, branches, leaves—perfect materials for this restful space!

256) Hug a Tree

❄️ 🌼 ☀️ 🍁 12+ months

🕐 2 minutes

Have you ever shut your eyes and hugged a tree? They are rough, hard, and silent. They are alive and connected to the nature that surrounds us. There are thousands of unique and special trees in every forest. Hugging them can help you learn how big life is!

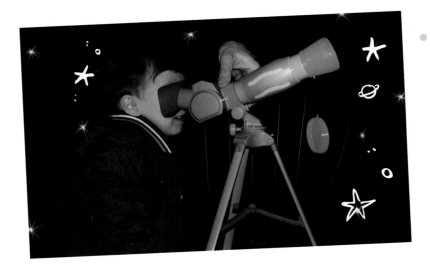

(257) Nighttime Excursion to See the Stars

❄ ☀ 3+ years

🕐 1 hour

Looking at the stars is always a good time to unplug, look at the sky, and open our minds. If you can escape for a night to a nearby mountain, away from noise and light pollution, do it! Seeing the stars in the night sky is a gift.

You can find a constellation guide on our website. See note on page 4.

(258) Clean the Beach or Forest

❄ ✽ ☀ 🍁 2–3+ years

🕐 25 minutes

The forest and the beach are beautiful, and it is important to take care of them. There are many ways to do our part to maintain them and keep them clean, like taking a day to pick up trash.

(259) Drawing in the Sand

❄ ✽ ☀ 🍁 12+ months

🕐 10 minutes

Sand is a beautiful canvas for writing messages and making drawings. A stick, a rock, or our hands and feet are great tools. The paintings you make in the sand are ephemeral, a perfect place to write secrets, confessions, messages of hope and our secret desires.

(260) Make a Wish on a Dandelion

🌼 **14+ months**

🕐 5 seconds

Dandelions are often considered weeds, and since they can be found everywhere, adults often don't pay them any attention. However, children find them much more fascinating to pick, observe, pluck, and blow on. Adults should follow the children's lead and observe these flowers, learning alongside the child in these special moments.

DID YOU KNOW?

The fluffy hairs of a dandelion are called "pappi."

(261) Storytelling on Rocks

❄️ 🌼 ☀️ 🍁 **2–3+ years**

🕐 20 minutes

Who says that good stories are only written on paper? You can create your own stories on rocks! Paint and draw on them, each one representing a different object, animal, or person until you have all the elements of your story. Keep them so you have these little works of art to reuse and tell other stories.

(262) How a Plant Breathes

❄ ✿ ☀ 🍁 **6+ years**

🕐 30 minutes

Plants, like all living things, need to breathe in order to live. You can check this by doing the following experiment: take a plant from your house and wrap a few of its leaves in a plastic bag. Leave it for a few hours, and you will see small drops of water in the plastic bag. This water is produced because, when a plant breathes, it absorbs oxygen and gives off carbon dioxide and water vapor; this is the sign that shows us that plants breathe and really are alive.

MATERIALS

- Small plastic bag

- Plant

DID YOU KNOW?

Plants don't only breathe with their leaves, but also through other openings in the bark of their stems called "lenticels," and also through their roots.

263 Natural Candle

❄ ✿ ☀ 🍁 4–5+ years

🕐 15 minutes

How can we create a natural candle? It is
very simple! And it is made from two common
ingredients you can find at home: a peeled banana
cut in half and a walnut. Put the walnut in the
banana so it is sticking out a little. Light the walnut,
and you've made a light!

264 What Are You Touching?

❄ ✿ ☀ 🍁 4–5+ years

🕐 15 minutes

Sometimes we take a walk without paying much
attention to the things around us. Using our senses,
we can perceive where we are going. A good way
to try concentrating on each element is with a very
simple method: close your eyes, and try, without the
sense of sight, to identify what you're touching. Is
it a tree, a flower, a rock? Nature is full of things to
discover!

265 Bury Your Feet in the Sand

☀ 12+ months

🕐 5 minutes

The beach is full of fun activities to connect you to your environment.
Bury or cover your feet with sand. You can observe if the sand is wet, hot,
if it is fine or thick. What do you feel with your feet buried in the sand?

(266) Go Sledding

❄ **4–5+ years**

🕐 10 minutes

Every season brings different experiences. One of the things that winter brings is snow. A getaway to somewhere snowy is always a good idea to enjoy these times of year, and bringing a sled can make it all the more fun!

(268) Observe Rocks

❄ 🌼 ☀ 🍁 **2+ years**

🕐 10 minutes

Rocks can provide us with endless activities. While you look at rocks, you can see what shape they are, what color they are, how much they weigh, which ones weigh more, what texture they have, etc.

(267) Make a Wreath of Leaves

❄ 🌼 ☀ 🍁 **2–3+ years**

🕐 15–20 minutes

For this activity, you will need cardboard, glue, string, flowers, leaves, fruits, etc. Cut a circle out of the cardboard. Put glue around the cardboard and stick the things you like to it. Once you are done, cut a string or cord and hang it wherever you like.

(269) Create a Sensory Walk

 ☀ 🍁 **18+ months**

🕐 30 minutes

To create a sensory nature walk, begin by clearing an area or setting a boundary with sticks, and make sections or areas. In each space, you can use different materials: in one you can put dry leaves on the ground, in another one you can put branches, in another one rocks or sand. The idea is to take your shoes off and walk in the circuit, feeling each element with your feet. It is an unbeatable experience!

(270) Have a Picnic

❄ ✿ ☀ 🍁 **2+ years**

🕐 20 minutes

A blanket, a basket, some food prepared with love, and a spot to enjoy it all are all the things you need. This is a great way to connect with nature, with the song of the birds, the air moving through the leaves of the trees, the breeze from the sea, or the silence—or the laughs! This is all you need!

(271) Make a Snow Man

❄ **2+ years**

🕐 20 minutes

Who hasn't made a snow man? Or at least tried? Once you have the snow, all you need is a carrot for the nose, two chestnuts or rocks for the eyes, sticks for the hair, and leaves for the tie. Use items like these from nature so that your impact on the environment is as small as possible.

(272) Visit a Nature Reserve

❄ ✿ ☀ 🍁 **2+ years**

🕐 1 hour

Nature reserves are places protected from humans with the intention of preserving the species and ecosystems that need attention. Visiting these places can teach us about certain species of animals and plants that we may not be familiar with and also how to protect our environment.

(273) Paint in the Snow

❄ **4–5+ years**

🕐 10 minutes

Painting with snow? Yes! But this painting will be 100 percent natural. For this activity, you will need a container to bring your homemade paint to wherever the snow is. To prepare your homemade paint, you will use cornstarch, food coloring, and water. Once these ingredients are mixed, you will have a thick mixture to paint with and the snow will be a perfect canvas!

(274) Visit a Farm

❄ ✿ ☀ 🍁 **12+ months**

🕐 20 minutes

Farms give us a great opportunity to be in contact with cows, horses, roosters, hens, goats, and other animals that you can visit with, observe, learn to respect and take care of. Farms give us, among other things, the opportunity to promote our autonomy and responsibility.

(275) Natural Feather Dusters

❄ ✿ ☀ 🍂 **2+ years**

🕐 10 minutes

Is there anything more beautiful than a natural feather duster? You can use them for tickling, a massage, for cleaning—all you need are some sticks, feathers, leaves or flowers, and tape. Collect a lot of feathers and leaves and tape them to the end of the stick. Now you're ready!

DID YOU KNOW?

Dust particles or lint quickly adhere to the duster. This is because they have the ability to be attracted to static electricity.

MATERIALS

- Sticks
- Feathers
- Leaves
- Flowers
- Tape

(276) Make an Air Freshener with Oranges and Cloves

❄ ✿ ☀ 🍁 3+ years

🕐 20 minutes

You can make an air freshener for your home, a closet, the bathroom, or the kitchen. All you need is an orange and some cloves. Yes, the spice. The idea is to stick the cloves into the orange in different shapes and patterns. Once they're decorated, you have a natural and environmentally friendly air freshener.

(277) Is it Windy?

❄ ✿ ☀ 🍁 2+ years

🕐 5 minutes

To see if the wind is blowing, you can put some pieces of tape on the branches of a tree and see if they move, and if they do, which way. If you want to add a special touch, you can use different colored strings, things with different textures and sizes, and hang all different kinds of things. When the wind blows, you'll have a real rainbow!

(278) Homemade Soap

❄ ✿ ☀ 🍁 4–5+ years

🕐 4 hours

The first thing to decide is what shape you want your soap to be, so you can pick a nice mold. Afterward, gather the ingredients you need: two small cups of shea butter, dried flowers and herbs, essential oils (whatever scents you like), and cocoa butter. Heat the shea butter and cocoa butter over a low flame, mixing until they are completely melted. When they're melted, take them off the heat, and add the dried herbs or flowers, and then once they are mixed, add a few drops of essential oil. Pour the mixture into the mold and put it in the fridge! Once four hours have passed, you can take it out of the mold, and you have a homemade bar of soap that you made with your own hands.

(279) Muddy Rainy Days

❄ ✿ ☀ 🍁 **12+ months**

🕐 15 minutes

Why do rainy days make us so sad? Let's turn it around! Normally you are stuck at home on these days and can't enjoy the experiences because of the rain. Get dressed in all your rain gear and let's go! Now you can splash and jump and get muddy without stopping!

(280) Yarn Sticks

❄ ✿ ☀ 🍁 **4+ years**

🕐 15 minutes

Next time you're on a nature walk, collect some sticks for this activity. The only other thing you need is yarn. The idea is to wrap the yarn around the sticks. You can alternate different colors. Once you're finished, this stick will have a ton of uses: a magic wand, drumsticks, a decorative object.

(281) Pinecone Hedgehogs

❄ ✿ ☀ 🍁 **2+ years**

🕐 10 minutes

You will need pinecones, clay, and small rocks. Press the clay around the end of the pinecone, and then stick two small rocks into it, making the eyes for the hedgehog. Put the third small rock between them for the nose and there you go! You have a little hedgehog.

(282) Breathe, Reconnect

❄ ✿ ☀ 🍂 **2+ years**

🕐 15 minutes

Breathing happens without us paying any attention, but sometimes you can stop and feel your breath as a way to feel present. Close your eyes and pay attention to the sounds around you. Reconnecting in this way is essential.

(283) Natural Textures

❄ ✿ ☀ 🍂 **3–4+ years**

🕐 5 minutes

You can find so many different shapes and textures in nature. A simple idea to explore nature is to take a piece of clay and press natural elements into it. You can see what kinds of textures and shapes show up in the impression.

(284) Building a Sand Castle

☀ **18+ months**

🕐 15 minutes

There are so many moments to share when you are at the beach in the summer. Children love building with sand. You can try coming together as a family to build a big castle. Will it stay up or will it fall?

285 Weaving with Natural Objects

❄ ✿ ☀ 🍁 **4–5+ years**

🕐 15 minutes

For this activity, you will need a piece of cardboard, yarn, and scissors. Make a grid with the yarn across the cardboard. Use this grid to weave with other natural objects that inspire you!

286 Hiking Route

❄ ✿ ☀ 🍁 **4+ years**

🕐 30 minutes

Plan a hiking route with your family, keeping everyone's age and ability in mind. Once you've chosen the right route, start walking and enjoy nature!

287 Sleep Under the Stars

☀ **6–7+ years**

🕐 8 hours

Lie on your back and look at the thousands of luminous points. There is nothing like it! All the beauty of a tiny, tiny piece of the universe right over your head. Observe, try to touch with your fingers, find constellations, tell stories, and enjoy the sky!

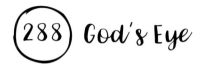

(288) God's Eye

❄ ✿ ☀ 🍁 **4+ years**

🕐 25 minutes

For this activity, you will need yarn of different colors and two sticks.

Tie the sticks together in the center while holding them next to each other. Turn them so they make a cross and continue winding the yarn around the sticks in whichever direction you want. Make sure the sticks are joined securely before continuing.

Wrap the yarn from front to back around the first stick, either clockwise or counterclockwise. You can decide which direction, but make sure you stay consistent when wrapping the sticks. Once you've wrapped the first stick, do the same at the next stick, and then the next. If you want to change colors, bring your current colored yarn to the back and tie the two colors together so the knot is not visible from the front. Continue on with the new color. You can use as many colors as you like.

DID YOU KNOW?

This craft originates from the Southwestern United States and is also called "Si'Kuli." People have been making these for over two thousand years. They were initially created as a symbol of protection at birth, saying that every year is another circle in the "eye of God." The history of this craft is very interesting, and your children would certainly love to learn more about it.

MATERIALS

- Different colors of yarn
- Two sticks
- Scissors

"Patience is a tree with a bitter root, but bears sweet fruits."

Persian Proverb

(289) Fireside Storytelling

❄ ✿ ☀ 🍁 **3+ years**

🕐 20 minutes

Fire is a magnetic element, mysterious and hypnotic. Everyone loves fire, especially children. Sitting around a fire, watching the flames, and telling stories is something that has been done since the beginning of time and brings people together. It creates bonds, harmony, and brings light and heat, which is so important on cold, dark nights. Nightfall is a time to relax, to let your worries take a back seat, and to put your thoughts into perspective. It is a time when our feelings surface, and maybe even the spiritual side of each person is open to connect with the moment. It is a great time to experience together and to share!

(290) Paintbrushes with Sticks & Natural Elements

❄ ✿ ☀ 🍁 **4–5+ years**

🕐 15–20 minutes

Nature is full of elements that we can use to encourage creativity. For this activity, you will need to collect sticks, flowers, and different kinds of leaves that you find on your excursions. And don't forget string! Tie your flowers and leaves to the end of the stick, making sure it is well secured. Use your new tools to paint and create art!

(291) Drawing Faces on Leaves

✿ ☀ 🍁 **18+ months**

🕐 5 minutes

For this activity, you'll be replacing paper with leaves and painting right on them. Using a marker, draw a mouth, a nose, eyes, and whatever other features you think would be on its face. Get inspiration from the people around you!

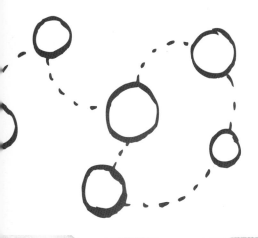

(292) Find a Tree

🌼 ☀ **4–5+ years**

🕐 20–25 minutes

This is a very simple activity. Take turns closing your eyes and looking for a tree. Once you find it, explore it! Touch it, hug it, smell it.

(293) Make Numbers on Rocks

❄ 🌼 ☀ 🍁 **4–5+ years**

🕐 25–30 minutes

There are so many activities you can do with rocks, and here you are going to paint numbers on them. You will need rocks and acrylic or tempera paint. You can also use oil-based markers that are used for painting on glass. First, you will need to wash the rocks. Once they are dry, use a pencil to draw a number, and then paint your drawing. Use your rocks to help with math, go shopping, or create riddles.

(294) Insect Refuge

❄ 🌼 ☀ 🍁 **5–6+ years**

🕐 30 minutes

Who says there can't be hospitals for bugs? Let's make a nice habitat they will like. To do this, you will need a flowerpot, sticks of all shapes and sizes, pinecones, bamboo sticks, pieces of wood, straw, leaves, whatever you can find outside will work. Collect all of these in the flowerpot on your lawn or in your yard. Bugs can help control pests and help pollinate plants. Earwigs, ladybugs, bees, and beetles are all friendly and helpful bugs. Depending on what materials you use, you will attract different insects.

(295) Watch the Sunset

❄ ✿ ☀ 🍂 **12+ months**

🕐 **15 minutes**

This activity helps children learn about the cycle of a day. There is no better way to track time than by observing the sky: nature's clock tells us it is getting dark, and this is a clear and physical moment that shows us the day is ending. You won't want to miss this event!

(296) Mud Dolls

✿ ☀ **2+ years**

🕐 **15 minutes**

Construct figures and dolls out of mud and other natural elements you find. All you need is a little water to mix into the dirt and you'll have mud to build with. This is a fun activity you can enjoy with the whole family.

(297) Flower Petal Garlands

✿ **4–5+ years**

🕐 **15–20 minutes**

Collect different kinds of leaves and flower petals. Take a walk outside and collect whatever catches your eye. Afterward, use a needle and thread to string your items together. You can make it as long as you want and decorate your house with these garlands.

(298) Bending water

❄ ✿ ☀ 🍁 **4–5+ years**

🕑 10 minutes

How can you bend water? It's very simple! You will need water, of course, and also a balloon and a towel. Run the water from the faucet, or if you can find a natural fountain, you can try this there, too. Rub the balloon on the towel a few times, and then hold the balloon close to the stream of water and see what happens. You'll have to try it to find out!

Hint: Electromagnetism

(299) See the Sunrise

❄ ✿ ☀ 🍁 **4–5+ years**

🕑 15 minutes

It is so worth it to get up early—even more when our schedules are very busy. Make a plan with the whole family to wake up early in the morning and go watch the sunrise. What a sight!

(300) Natural Colors

❄ ✿ ☀ 🍁 **2+ years**

🕑 20–25 minutes

Imagine making colors from natural elements! All you need are a few different things to make colors. You will need some white paint in different containers, so you can add each element until it is the color you want. Try this with ground rosemary, pepper, turmeric, cinnamon, and coco, for example. Now you are ready to paint and explore your artistic spirit! Remember that earth tones are beautiful.

(301) Biodegradation

☀ **4–5+ years**

🕐 **1 week**

Taking care of our environment is very important. Finding ways to do this with your family is very helpful. One idea is to work as a family to recycle and compost, trying this experiment to see what happens to different materials in this process.

For this activity, you will need small, biodegradable flowerpots and different materials you use every day. Put one kind of material in each flowerpot, sorting by whether it is packaging, organic material, or whatever other kind of thing you want to try this with. Next, you will find somewhere to bury these flowerpots with the intention of returning in a week. Mark the place where you buried them with a sign. Dig up your pots after a week and observe what each material has done and what items were biodegradable. Some items may still be completely intact.

You can also take this opportunity to research how long different materials take to degrade, or how earthworms consume organic material and turn it into soil.

You can find a worksheet that shows the length of time it takes objects to biodegrade on our website. See note on page 4.

MATERIALS

- Small, biodegradable flowerpots
- Different kinds of waste: plastic, organic waste, glass, cardboard

"Only when the last tree has died, the last river has been poisoned, and the last fish has been caught, will we realize we cannot eat money."

Cree Proverb

DID YOU KNOW?

Organic waste creates a kind of soil called "compost" that is very nutritious for plants.

(302) Observing Tadpoles in a Puddle

🌼 2+ years

🕐 15 minutes

Have you ever watched tadpoles swim in a puddle? This is a simple activity but a great opportunity to stop, look, and observe, thinking about how one day they will grow feet. These are observations that help teach children about growth.

(303) Enjoy a Rainbow

❄️ 🌼 ☀️ 🍁 4–5+ years

🕐 15 minutes

Rainbows aren't something we see every day, since the conditions aren't always right. Sometimes, after a rainstorm, you'll be surprised to see a rainbow in the sky. This helps us remember that the sun always comes out after the rain.

(304) Observing Spiderwebs

❄️ 🌼 ☀️ 🍁 2+ years

🕐 20 minutes

Spiderwebs are not always easy to see. Sometimes, if they are backlit, you can see them better, but it is still hard to see the details. How can you make this easier? Try taking a piece of black cardboard and attaching it to a stick with some tape. Here is our magnifying glass for spiderwebs! Hold it behind the spiderweb so you can observe the details.

305 Tracing the Shadow of a Tree

✿ ☀ **4+ years**

🕐 5 minutes

For this activity, you will need to use your imagination to think about different ways to draw in nature. What are some ways you can think of that use natural materials? Rocks, sticks, plants, and flowers can all be used to create the silhouette.

306 Make a Mud Painting

❄ ✿ ☀ 🍂 **12+ months**

🕐 20 minutes

You will need a canvas, brushes, and soil. You could collect different kinds of dirt on your next nature walk. Bring them back to your house for this activity. Then all you need to do is mix them with water and try painting. How does sand look when you use it as paint? How about the soil from a mountain? Are they the same? Experiment with these natural pigments!

307 Make Lavender Perfume

✿ **4+ years**

🕐 20 minutes

Making perfume is a fun activity. You will need lavender, scissors, distilled water, a small funnel, small bottles, and alcohol. Cut the lavender and put it in a mortar with a little bit of water and grind it. Using a funnel, put this mixture into a bottle with three tablespoons of alcohol and one tablespoon of water. Decorate your bottle with some little lavender leaves to give it a special touch, and now you have a perfect perfume!

308 Use a Tree as an Easel

☀ **3+ years**

🕐 **15–20 minutes**

Tape a piece of paper to a tree. The tree will be our easel, helping inspire us on our journey through nature. Have you ever tried painting outside? It is a great experience!

309 Make a Solar Clock

❄ ✿ ☀ 🍁 **7+ years**

🕐 **1 day**

Don't worry! You don't need to be an engineer to make a clock! The one we're making will use a natural motor: the sun. All you need is a stick, some rocks, and most importantly, a sunny place that doesn't have any shade.

Once you have all of your materials, you'll put the stick upright in the ground. See where it casts its shadow and place a rock at the end of the shadow. As the shadow moves due to the movement of the sun, continue placing rocks to record these movements. When you come back the next day, continue to do this until the sun is back in its original spot. Once you have all of the rocks placed on the ground, you can mark them with chalk and use this as a clock. What time is it?

310 Play with Water Toys in a Puddle

❄ ✿ ☀ 🍁 **2+ years**

🕐 **15 minutes**

This is a great opportunity to enjoy the little things. Rain may seem boring, but who says we have to stay home? Let's go out and play in the water! The puddles left behind by a rainstorm are so much fun. Take out your waterproof toys and bring them along. You can enjoy this moment in nature and play in the puddles and mud.

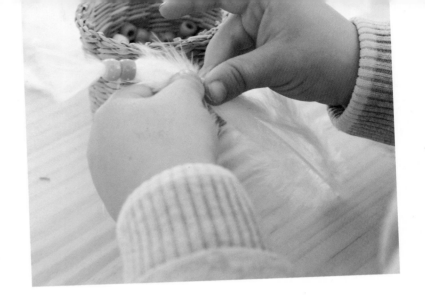

311 Decorate Feathers with Beads

❄ ✿ ☀ 🍃 **2+ years**

🕐 15 minutes

Feathers are easy to find. Collect some on your walks for this activity. Take some beads and string them onto the feather. This is a nice way to decorate them!

312 Look for the First Signs of Spring

❄ ✿ **4–5+ years**

🕐 15 minutes

As winter fades into spring, the world is full of different signs that signal the change of season. Sometimes it is a plant beginning to grow, melting snow, or a flower beginning to bloom. It's time to observe and discover!

313 Draw on a Mirror in Nature

✿ ☀ **3–4+ years**

🕐 10 minutes

This is a special and fun activity. Bring a mirror, some paper, and some tempera paints in different colors to whatever site you enjoy in nature. Put the mirror on the ground or against a tree. Observe what you see in the mirror, and try to paint what is reflected. Try this with the whole family so you can see how each person sees the world.

(314) Chlorophyll Experiment

 ✿ ☀ 🍁 **3–4+ years**

🕐 15 minutes

Collect different colored leaves and boil them for five minutes. Fill multiple glasses with alcohol. Take your leaves out of the boiling water with tongs and put each one in a different glass.

Compare the differences, if there are any. The longer you leave them in the glass, the more intense their colors will become. Are they all the same?

MATERIALS

- Pot of water
- Different colored leaves
- Alcohol
- 3 or 4 small glasses
- Tongs

DID YOU KNOW?

Chlorophyll helps plants and trees with the process of photosynthesis. Not only that, but it is also what makes leaves green. Other living things like algae also have a lot of chlorophyll in them.

(315) Shapes and Plates

✿ ☀ **2+ years**

🕐 10 minutes

Use your paper plates left over from snack to make a magnifying glass to help us focus on details around us. Cut a hole in your plate and tape it to a stick and there you go!

(316) Climb a Bale of Hay

✿ ☀ 🍁 **2+ years**

🕐 5 minutes

When you're driving on a trip, if you see a bale of hay, why not stop and check it out if it's not on private property? Climb it, touch it, and smell it!

(317) Leaf Skewers

✿ ☀ **4+ years**

🕐 10 minutes

You will need skewers and leaves. Stick the skewer in the ground so it is sticking straight up. Take your leaves and spear them with the skewer until it is full. A beautiful work of art in nature!

318 Balancing on Tree Trunks

  3–4+ years

🕐 10 minutes

When you're walking through the woods, sometimes you'll find tree trunks that have fallen. Try practicing balancing while you walk across one!

319 Keep an Apple from Oxidizing

 4–5+ years

🕐 24 hours

When you peel an apple, it turns brown after a while. But what can you do to keep that from happening? Let's investigate! Slice an apple and put the slices in different receptacles. To each receptacle, add a little of one of the following: lemon juice, milk, orange juice, and water, and leave one receptacle with just the apple slices and no liquid. After 24 hours, see which liquid was the most effective at keeping the apple from oxidizing. What do you think it will be?

320 Color a Picture and Leave It in the Rain

  2–3+ years

🕐 10 minutes

This is a great activity to help you look at the bright side, and to not let the rain stop you! For this activity, draw with crayons on a piece of paper in whatever colors you like, then leave it out in the rain. See how the colors combined when the paper became wet.

(321) Ice Cream Sundaes with Dirt, Flowers & Leaves

❀ ☼ 🍁 **4–5+ years**

🕐 **10 minutes**

Let's make ice cream sundaes out of mud, flowers, and leaves. Make your own combination of elements you can find in nature. This is just for playing pretend and not for eating!

(322) Mystery Bag

❄ ❀ ☼ 🍁 **3–4+ years**

🕐 **15–20 minutes**

How many times have you passed a field of flowers without stopping to smell them? How many times have you seen a tree and not stopped to touch its bark? In this activity, you are going to pay attention to the details nature has to offer. You'll need a blindfold and some objects from nature that fit in a bag: pinecones, sticks, leaves, flowers, acorns, nuts, etc. The person wearing the blindfold will put their hand in the sack, take out an object, and try to guess what it is. You can use all your senses except for sight!

(323) Sensory Bottles

❄ ❀ ☼ 🍁 **10+ months**

🕐 **15–20 minutes**

When you are taking a nature walk, you can always find objects that have fallen on the ground. Collect these items and put them in a bottle. In one bottle, you can collect acorns, in another, a branch of pine needles, in another, some sticks or rocks, whatever you want! You can shake them to see what sounds they make, or put water in them and see how they become magnified, and explore and experiment with all of your senses.

324 Potpourri Bags

❄️ 🌼 ☀️ 🍁 **2+ years**

🕐 15 minutes

Potpourri bags are perfect to put in a drawer to bring a little nature into your home. They are very easy to make. You will need dry lavender and rosemary, a container, a spoon, and some cloth bags. Use the spoon to put the rosemary or lavender into the bag and close it. That's it!

325 Singing in the Rain

❄️ 🌼 ☀️ 🍁 **2+ years**

🕐 10 minutes

Life is too serious to add even more drama. If it is raining, go out, sing, laugh, and dance!

326 Dehydrate Fruit

❄️ 🌼 ☀️ 🍁 **3+ years**

🕐 4 hours

Who says fruit snacks can't be healthy? Make your own with real fruit! Set your oven to 130°F (55°C) and cut the fruits you want to dry: bananas, strawberries, oranges, apples, raspberries, whatever you like. Put parchment paper on a baking sheet and place your fruit slices in a single layer. Leave them in the oven for 4 to 6 hours, and you will have your fruit candies ready at the end of the day!

(327) Make a Bird Feeder

 4–5+ years

 15 minutes

Food for birds can be scarce in the winter, and it is harder for them to find what they need to eat. You can make a simple bird feeder with a piece of orange peel left over from making juice or a salad, nuts and seeds, and a piece of string.

Mix the seeds in a bowl and make four holes in the orange peel: two on one side and two on the other, to help make an "orange bowl." Run the string through these holes so you can hang it up, and fill it with the seed mix!

MATERIALS

- An orange peel
- Different kinds of seeds (oats, sunflower seeds, peanuts, breadcrumbs)
- A piece of string

DID YOU KNOW?

Birds are born with a tooth to help them break the eggshell as they come out. It falls out a few days after they are born.

TWEET
TWEET

TWEET
TWEET

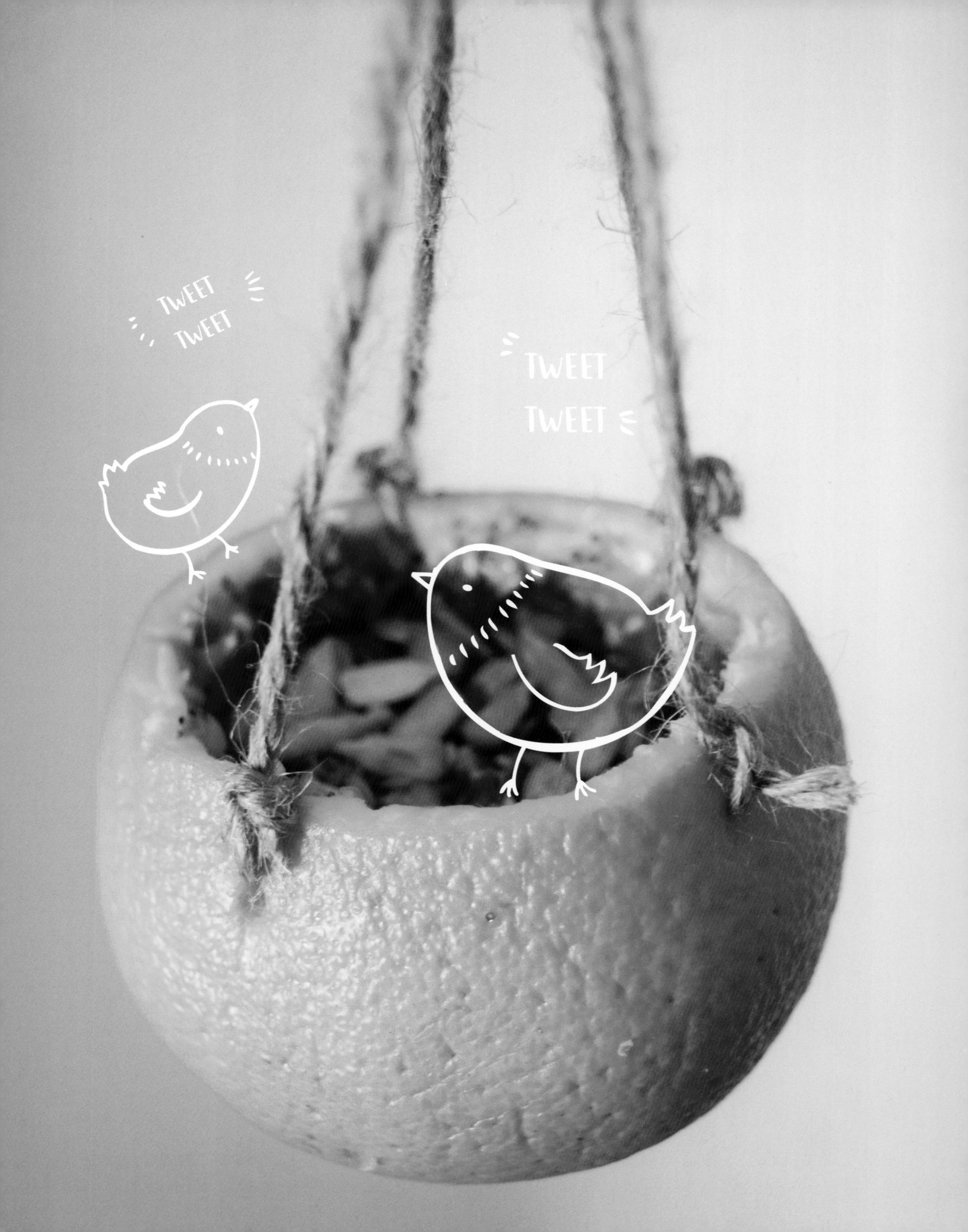
TWEET
TWEET
TWEET
TWEET

328 Orange Peel Candle Holder

❄ ✿ ☀ 🍁 **4–5+ years**

🕐 15 minutes

What's better than a nice scent? Especially when it is accompanied by the soft light of a candle. For this activity, you're going to be making candles in orange peels. Cut an orange in half and scoop the fruit out with a spoon. Cut it into whatever shape you want, and then set your candle inside.

329 Mud Cakes

✿ ☀ **3–4+ years**

🕐 10 minutes

Taking a walk on a rainy day to a trail nearby can be a lot of fun for children and for adults who want to embrace their inner child, sharing mud pies and cakes with their children. This is fun for everyone! Enjoy the moment and the smell of the mud fresh from the rain.

330 Measure Rain with a Cup

❄ ✿ ☀ 🍁 **2+ years**

🕐 5 minutes

Rain is a great resource for learning. Try timing how long it takes to fill a glass with rain, or seeing how much rain fills the glass in 15 minutes!

331 Water the Garden

❄ ✿ ☼ 🍁 **18+ months**

🕐 10 minutes

Not everyone has a garden, but see if you know anyone who does who will let you come by and help and learn a little bit. Or you can find a public garden to visit near your house that will let you come by and work and observe.

332 Grow Seasonal Fruits & Vegetables

❄ ✿ ☼ 🍁 **2+ years**

🕐 20 minutes

Planting vegetables and watching them grow is an interesting process: seeds don't grow right away, and you will need lots of care and patience. After you have planted them, you'll need to fertilize them, water them regularly, and fix any problems that come up. This is a great opportunity to learn about this process.

333 Harvest Your Garden

✿ ☼ 🍁 **2+ years**

🕐 15 minutes

Once you have grown some plants, it is time to harvest the fruits of your labor. Seeing these results is a great joy. Pick fruits carefully and make a meal with them to enjoy as a family. To eat something you have grown yourself with your own hands is an amazing feeling.

(334) Collect Treasures from Nature in an Egg Carton

❄ ✿ ☀ 🍁 **2+ years**

🕐 15–20 minutes

For this activity, all you need is an egg carton. Use this to collect and store the treasures you find in nature!

(335) Find Objects in Nature that Match in Color

❄ ✿ ☀ 🍁 **18+ months**

🕐 15 minutes

When you are out on a nature walk, it is fun to create challenges that help us pay closer attention to our surroundings. For example, pick a color and find objects that all match that color and collect them in a bag where you can look at them all together. Nature is full of colors for you to discover!

(336) Citrus Necklace

❄ ✿ ☀ 🍁 **2+ years**

🕐 4 hours

For this activity, you will need a variety of oranges and lemons, parchment paper, thread, and a knife. Cut the citrus fruits into thin rings, and put them in a bowl with lemon juice for 30 minutes. Prepare a cookie sheet with a piece of parchment paper, and turn the oven to 185°F (85°C). Dry the citrus slices with a paper towel and arrange them in a single layer on the cookie sheet. Put them in the oven for 4 hours until they are dry. Once they are cooled and dry, string them on the thread by the middle and make your necklace.

(337) Object Search Game

❄️ 🌼 ☀️ 🍁 **2+ years**

🕐 20–25 minutes

For this game, make a list of things to look for when you go to the mountains or the beach. This can be an illustrated list or a written list, with clues for everyone to find. Let's explore!

You can find a list of ideas on our website. See note on page 4.

(338) Jump in the Leaves

🍁 **2+ years**

🕐 5 minutes

When you're walking in the woods during the fall, you'll find a blanket of multicolored leaves covering the ground. Scoop these leaves into a giant pile and jump right into them. This only takes five minutes and is really fun.

(339) Nature Collage

❄️ 🌼 ☀️ 🍁 **4–5+ years**

🕐 15 minutes

Collect objects from nature that catch your eye and put them in a basket. Take whatever sized paper you want and glue or tape your objects in a design that you like.

(340) Wash Apples

❄ ✿ ☼ 🍁 **12+ months**

🕐 15 minutes

Washing fruit can be fun, especially when you do it with your whole family. A brush and a bucket of water is all you need to get ready to make those apples shine. Use warm water to help clean the dirt off them.

DID YOU KNOW?

Most apples are grown in temperate climates like those of Europe, the United States, and Asia.

MATERIALS

- Brush
- Bucket
- Apples
- Water

"One bad apple can spoil the bunch."

Proverb

(341) Tic-Tac-Toe in Nature

❄ ✿ ☼ 🍁 **4–5+ years**

🕐 5 minutes

To create a Tic-Tac-Toe board, you will need four sticks and six natural objects, for example, three pinecones and three pieces of bark. Place two sticks vertically and the other two sticks horizontally to form a grid with spaces between the sticks. Once you have your grid, you're ready to play this rustic game!

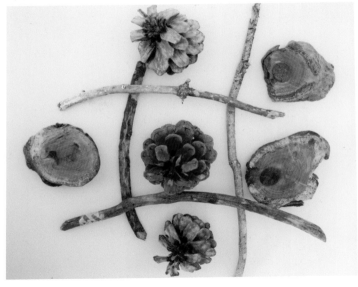

(342) Nature Mobile

❄ ✿ ☼ 🍁 **4–5+ years**

🕐 20–25 minutes

Making a mobile to hang in your house is a very fun activity. All you need is a stick, colored thread or fishing line, and some objects from nature: leaves, flowers, sticks, pinecones. Attach the objects to the stick with the thread and hang them at different lengths. Hang it in your window so the objects move when the wind blows.

Another nice thing about a mobile is that it never runs out of batteries, never loses its signal, and, of course, it doesn't have a screen.

(343) Ice Wreath

❄ ✿ ☼ 🍁 **2+ years**

🕐 3 hours

You've heard of wreaths made of sticks or leaves, but ice? It's very simple to make. You will need a silicon ring mold, water, and objects from nature. Fill the mold with water and put your natural objects in. Put it in the freezer for a few hours, and once it is ready, you can hang it by a string on your door or in your garden and see how long it lasts.

344) Go Camping

❄ ✿ ☀ 🍁 **2+ years**

🕐 1–2 days

The whole family will enjoy the freedom of a camping trip, getting to know people, playing, and exploring your creativity and potential!

345) Swim in a River

☀ **2+ years**

🕐 10 minutes

Swimming in a river is an experience everyone should have. These are very different from the city pool you may be used to, enjoying the beautiful scenery and views in an incredible paradise.

346) Planets Orbiting the Sun

❄ ✿ ☀ 🍁 **6+ years**

🕐 20 minutes

Draw a circle in the sand about 13 feet in diameter and draw a straight line that divides it in half by the circumference. One person will be the sun and stand in the middle of the circle. The other people will be the planets and stand on the line that runs through the circle. In this game, the sun tries to catch the planets without moving from the circumference line. They must always have a hand or foot on the line. The planets can move in circles to avoid being caught.

(347) Grow a Seed

❄ ✿ ☀ 🍁 2–3+ years

🕐 7 days

This is an easy experiment. You will need a legume like a chickpea, a bean, or a lentil, a glass bottle, and a cotton ball soaked with water. Put the seed in the wet cotton ball and put it in the glass bottle. Leave this in a window, and if everything goes well, you will see a tiny sprout in a couple of days. It is important that the cotton ball remain wet, so make sure you add a little water every day until your sprout is big enough to plant in a flower pot.

(348) Find a Cicada Shell

☀ 3–4+ years

🕐 10 minutes

Is there a sound that represents summer more than the sound of the cicadas? They fill the trees and rub their wings making that specific sound. When cicadas grow, they molt, leaving their old skin behind so they can grow bigger. You can find these shells all over the ground by the trees where they live.

VROOOOOM

(349) Ride a Tractor

❄ ✿ ☀ 🍁 2+ years

🕐 5 minutes

If you live in a city, you may not have had a lot of opportunities to see a tractor. Try to find a more rural area where you can see the different kinds of vehicles that are used on farms. Maybe you can ask some questions about these vehicles like, what does a tractor do? What are its wheels like? How many people can fit?

350 Skipping Stones

❄ ✾ ☀ 🍁 **2+ years**

🕐 5 minutes

Throwing rocks at the water to see if they will skip requires a specific skill: how you hold the rock in your hand, how you throw it, and choosing the right rock (nice and flat). If you don't get it on the first try, keep practicing until you get one right. See how far you can make it go!

351 Cartwheels in a Meadow

❄ ✾ ☀ 🍁 **14+ months**

🕐 1 minute

Isn't this tempting? Imagine a giant meadow, full of grass, where you can skip, do cartwheels, and dance. This doesn't have to be a fantasy—make it a reality!

352 Collect Sunflower Seeds

❄ ✾ ☀ 🍁 **3+ years**

🕐 15 minutes

Sunflowers are special flowers that turn to follow the sun. This is where they get their name. They bear delicious seeds, so if you can find a sunflower filled with seeds, you can pick them. What a treat!

(353) Recycle Paper

❄ ✿ ☼ 🍁 **2+ years**

🕐 8–9 hours

Cut paper into small pieces, and blend them up in the blender. Add water bit by bit until you have a thick mixture. After you take them out, spread them on a towel. Lay another towel on top and press to squeeze out the extra water. While it's still wet, add some flowers, leaves, or other materials you have on hand.

Leave it to dry, and once the water has evaporated you have a beautiful piece of recycled paper!

"Recycling isn't our obligation, it is our responsibility."

Anonymous

DID YOU KNOW?

Twenty-eight thousand trees are cut down every day to make toilet paper.

MATERIALS

- Used paper
- Newspaper
- Water
- Leaves
- Flowers
- Dehydrated fruit
- A blender
- A bowl
- Cloth or a filter
- A frame

(354) Puddles at the Beach

❄ ✿ ☀ 🍁 **18+ months**

🕐 15 minutes

You can often find large puddles by the sea. Why not play in them? It's time to jump, get wet, and laugh!

(355) Take a Walk in a Grove

❄ ✿ ☀ 🍁 **18+ months**

🕐 15 minutes

Groves are beautiful places where you can take a walk, play, lie down, or relax. Sometimes you don't need anything extra to enjoy the moment.

(356) Popcorn Garlands for the Birds

❄ **4+ years**

🕐 15 minutes

This is a simple activity! You only need thread and popcorn. String the popcorn on the thread, and you can hang these from the trees for the birds in the winter!

357 Visit a Bird Observatory

 5–6+ years

 2 hours

Herons, ducks, cormorants, and seagulls. For this activity, you will need binoculars and a place where you can observe birds. Learn about the different birds that live in this area, what they eat, where they live, what they are called, and other questions you may have in advance of visiting the observatory.

358 Dress a Tree

 2+ years

 15 minutes

Wrap yarn around a tree and hang different gifts from the string: leaves, small branches, or flowers. This is a fun way to interact with nature by touching it, smelling it, and hugging it!

359 Ride in a Canoe

 9+ months

 10 minutes

It is always fun to take a ride in a canoe! It can be very relaxing to float on the water this way!

(361) Walk in a Cornfield

❄ ✿ ☀ 🍁 9+ months

🕐 10 minutes

Taking a family trip to a cornfield is a great way to explore and learn about this vegetable. You can even find a corn maze where you need to test your cleverness to try to find the right way out.

(360) Celebrate Earth Day

✿ 2+ years

🕐 20 minutes

We have to care for our planet every day. On April 22, however, we commemorate how important it is to respect the Earth because it is our home and that of all living beings. Celebrating this day can be done in many ways. What if we do it by contributing to saving the Earth? Picking up waste from the ground, planting a tree, riding our bikes instead of taking the car, and pampering the planet as much as we can.

(362) Observe Fish

❄ ✿ ☀ 🍁 14 + months

🕐 5 minutes

Visiting a river or the ocean can give you the opportunity to observe fish in their natural habitat. All you need is five minutes to watch them. Where are they going? What color are they? What are they doing?

363 Climb Rocks

❄ ✿ ☀ 🍁 **3+ years**

🕐 10 minutes

Once small children learn to walk, they start to want to explore and see wherever they can go. Let's give them some safe opportunities to do so!

364 Collect Mountain Plants

❄ ✿ ☀ 🍁 **2+ years**

🕐 25 minutes

A walk is a great opportunity to see new things. In this case, you can try to pick plants and flowers you don't see in your backyard. All you need is a basket. Let's go!

365 Walnut Shell Necklaces

❄ ✿ ☀ 🍁 **3+ years**

🕐 25 minutes

These make great gifts for everyone in the family, and they are very easy to make: you will need two halves of the walnut shell and a string to connect them. If you want, you can give it a special touch and put a little treasure inside like a bell or a lucky coin and seal the shell shut.

About Us

ZAZU NAVARRO

Since she was a little girl, Zazu has been interested in the social aspects of life, which led her to study Social Education. Committed to creating positive change in society, she began her career as an educator of people of functional diversity. She started her beautiful family with Sergi, welcoming little Mafaldo into the world, and things began to make sense. Everything starts in infancy! Enthralled by the nature of childhood, she embarked on new studies that gave her the opportunity to become a Montessori guide and a Positive Discipline certified family educator. Since then, she has not stopped learning and sharing with others the importance of respectful learning on her blog **www.aprendiendoconmontessori.com**. She believes that the family is the best school you will find in your life. She dedicates her energy to learning, respecting, and accompanying her own family. Zazu is convinced that education for peace is possible if everyone participates in their own home.

TERESA CEBRIÁN

Teresa hopes to make everyone smile with her illustrations and to encourage their imagination to soar with the feelings they had in childhood. In her other profession, she is a user experience designer, where her goal is to make sure people using applications she designs will continue to use them. Thanks to the autumn elf and to Pepe and her beautiful family, she can combine these two professions that share something in common: looking to make life a little easier and more cheerful for people. Her main motivation is to put love and care into the things she does so that tomorrow everything is a little bit better.

Acknowledgments

DID YOU KNOW?

Gratitude improves relationships between people and creates empathy when it is done as a natural act and not as an obligation.

Thanks to **you** for reading this book while thinking about your family and yourself. For choosing to dedicate time to your family.

Thanks to **my family, my son** for showing me the path of love is the most pure, for giving me wings and the opportunity to be a better version of myself every day. To **my partner** because we are a team, and this makes it easier to be a parent.

Thank you to **my group Creciendo Criando** because there is nothing that brings me more pleasure than seeing your families playing together with your children.

Thank you to **Vicky, Silvia, Nuria, Ana, Esther, Wal, Estefi, Lorena, Fany** and **Olaya** for your beautiful, real, sincere friendship, and for being a shelter on this path of parenting.

Thank you to **Candi** and **Jose Antonio** for being family and helping. Thank you to **Toni** for your kindness and words that always make me reflect and grow.

Thank you to **my mother** and **my sister** for making my life complete, for teaching me the value of being a woman and for the infinite laughs when we are together. Thank you to **my father** for your light and all the memories that have stayed with me.

Thank you to **my grandmother** and **my grandfather** for sharing their toys, their childhood. Your memories are a treasured inheritance.

Thank you to **Teresa Cebrián** for creating part of this precious project. For your humility, your vision, and your passion for everything you do. For being a friend, confidant, support and spirit. Thank you to your **autumn elf** and to **Pepe**, because both have been such an important part of the process of this book.

Thank you to the beautiful **community of the blog Aprendiendo con Montessori** for believing that another kind of education is possible, for taking a bet on respect, peace, and love.

Zazu Navarro

Endless thanks to **my mother**, the strongest person I know, for your HUGE help with every detail. Thank you, Mom!

Another load of thanks to my best friend, lover and partner, my husband **Pepe**, for your support in every way. Defender to the death of the correct use of punctuation, I only hope you don't find too much to change after reading this book. (You'll tell me I only need to change a comma, while crying with pride.)

Thank you to **Zazu Navarro** for showing me that another form of education can be possible, and for trusting me with this project and with those to come.

AND THANK YOU to **my autumn elf**, for being the most beautiful baby in the world (I know, I'm not objective, but I have many witnesses that would say the same), and for teaching me to be my best self every day.

Teresa Cebrián